BEYOND THE HEBREW LEXICON

BEYOND THE HEBREW LEXICON

HEBREW LEXICON

LEARN TO DO HEBREW WORDS
STUDIES THAT TAKE YOU BEYOND
YOUR LEXICON

CHAIM BENTORAH

ISBN-13: 9781508601036

TABLE OF CONTENTS

INTRODUCTION

This book is a guide in how to do a Hebrew word study. However, in order to understand the ways and means of doing a Hebrew word study one needs to really understand not only the Hebrew language but the nature of the Semitic languages itself. As a teacher of the Biblical Hebrew language in a Bible College it was my job to maintain the highest academic standards for my students who were to be future pastors, missionaries and Christian teachers. This meant that I would follow a more traditional line of instruction which involved heavy memorization of Hebrew verbal forms and vocabulary.

However, I am now teaching outside the academic community where I am showing Christians of all backgrounds and educational experiences how to use the Hebrew language in their own personal Bible study. This means I am teaching people who are not interested in a grade or earning a degree but only to be able to study the Bible in the original language. This meant that I needed to give these people a tool which they could not only use in their personal study but that they could use it almost immediately without years of memorization and study. I have found that most people are really not interested in grammar so much as the study of a Hebrew word itself. Hence much of my time in teaching Hebrew is really spent in teaching them how to do a word study. Therefore, I have written this book for those who are not seeking an academic degree, nor wish to learn to speak Hebrew or to take a placement test for graduate school but only for those who wish to study the Word of God and find a richer and deeper understanding by peering into the ancient Hebrew language and studying a particular word.

This book is the result of my many years of research to develop a Bible study tool where any Christian, regardless of his age, educational background, or culture will be able to study the Word of God in the original language and go beyond a simple search in Strong's Concordance, a lexicon or their Bible Dictionary. This Bible study tool takes you beyond the lexicon and uses an ancient method of opening up each Hebrew word and reading it's *built in commentary.* This commentary is discovered by combining the ancient, esoteric structure of each Hebrew letter and translating a particular Hebrew word, letter by letter.

Less than fifty years ago there were very few English translations of the Bible other than the King James Version. Most people grew up reading the King James Version of the Bible and never questioned its accuracy. Most would even shun the few other translations as just a perversion of the Authorized Version of the Bible. As we entered into the second half of the twentieth century there was a literal explosion of new and modern translations of the Bible which were coming into common use among evangelical Christians and churches. Suddenly Christians came to the realization that the Bible is a translated work from two ancient and dead languages, Greek and Hebrew and that there can be many variations as to how words and whole passages of the Bible could be rendered.

As a teacher of the Classical Hebrew the most common question I am asked concerns which translation of the Bible is the correct translation or the most accurate translation. As all our modern English translations have been translated by skilled linguist and language scholars, I can only reply that all of these translations are good. This is then followed with the question as to why there are so many different renderings.

This is a difficult question if we consider it from a Western mindset. Our culture is a very scientific and mathematical culture where two plus two must always equal four. Thus, in our Western mindset there can only be one true rendering for every word in the Bible or it just cannot be the inspired, inerrant Word of God.

This book is not intended to argue for the inspiration and inerrancy of the Word of God. This will be accepted as a truth. What this book will attempt to do is point out that with regard to the Hebrew language as the original language of the Old Testament one word can have a wide range of meanings within the modern context of the English language.

Classical Hebrew died out during the captivity period around the sixth century BC and was only retained as a ceremonial language until the turn of the 20th Century when it was revived for use as a national language in Israel. However, what is spoken in Israel today is a modern version of Hebrew containing a couple hundred thousand words as opposed to the Classical Hebrew which has only about seventy five hundred words. Many of the original meaning of these words have been lost and what we have are just our traditional understandings of these words as they have been passed down from generation to generation. Even with the traditional understanding of a word, to find a modern English word that best fits an ancient word can be difficult. For instance at the beginning of the 20th Century we could have rendered the Hebrew word *ashar* as gay. That is *gay* in the sense of being happy and joyful. In the 21st Century if we were to render *ashar* as *gay* we would not be thinking of one's emotional state but of one's sexual orientation.

This constant change and evolutionary nature of a language, even over a relatively short period of time, gives us a need for continual revisions of former English translations of the Bible as well as entirely new versions. Yet with so many modern English versions of the Bible to choose from, how can we be sure which one conveys the correct understand of a word or verse?

One purpose of this book is to address this question and present an argument that the Word of God was written in the ancient Hebrew language under the inspiration of God for a very specific purpose. The very nature of the ambiguity of an ancient dead language allows for a variety of renderings for one specific word. It is true that we must apply proper linguistical, exegetical, and grammatical rules regarding proper syntax as well as an understanding of a word in its proper context but also in the context of the culture and text itself. Thus, merely looking a word up in the back of Strong's Concordance or a Bible Dictionary will not give you the entire understanding. You must also study the context of the passage and the cultural environment from which the passage was written.

This has been done with all our modern translations and yet you will still find many variations of renderings and some which are even of a conflicting or contradictory nature. There is an old Rabbinical tale of a man who asked his rabbi a question. The rabbi gave a very learned answer and the man excitedly declared, "You're right." Another rabbi overhearing the conversation gave an entirely different and contradictory answer. The man responded, "You're right." A third rabbi looked at the man and said, "He's right and he's right, they both cannot be right." The man looked at the third rabbi and said, "You're right." The point of the story is that in our culture we cannot accept two different answers as right, especially if they are a seeming contradiction. Yet, in the Semitic mindset, that is really no problem. The ancient Semitic mindset was not as complicated and exacting as our Western scientific and mathematical thought process.

I have written a book based upon the ancient Talmudic belief that there are *seventy faces of Torah*[1] In other words every verse in the Bible can have seventy shades of meaning and yet one meaning. When I was teaching an advanced Hebrew class in Bible college every year for the thirteen years I taught that class we would spend the first two months translating Proverbs 3:5-6. Every year there would be at least one student who would shed new light on this passage of Scripture that I had never considered. Generally this came from one of my international students who represented a different cultural background and experience. Such experiences and cultural input into a translation did not produce a wrong or a mistranslation but one which gave deeper insight into the message God was presenting in the passage. The Bible is a well that will never run dry. Every verse, ever word and even every letter is inspired by God to teach something about His relationship with us and our relationship with Him.

This book will present a means of doing a Hebrew word study where anyone, regardless of their educational background, cultural experience or level of spiritual maturity can study the Word of God in the original Hebrew. It is the purpose of this book to show that God has put a commentary into each word in the Hebrew so that He can speak to each person on an individual basis. I will show how anyone who so desires can open up this commentary without years of Hebraic studies and not only enter into a deeper understanding of Scripture but an understanding of a personal application that the Spirit of God will provide. You will learn how to move beyond just looking up a word in a Bible Dictionary or your lexicon and actually begin translating not only word for word but letter by letter using the ancient rabbinical esoteric meanings behind each letter of the Hebrew Alphabet.

---

[1] Rabbi Benjamin Blech, The Secrets of the Hebrew Words (Jason Aronson, Inc) page x

CHAPTER ONE
THE HISTORY OF THE HEBREW ALPHABET

The History of Language

We cannot speak with certainty as to how languages developed. Modern linguists do concluded that all of the languages on earth come from one universal language.[2] As to the exact nature of this language, that is consider unknown. Among Orthodox Jews and a rising school of thought known as Edenics, it is believe that God *hotwired* man's brain at creation to be fluid in a language which was Semitic in its nature and was most likely Hebrew.

As one who believes the Bible to be the inspired word of God, I would have to accept the fact that the whole world spoke one language up to the time of Babel when God confused the language of man and cause men to speak different languages.[3] This being the case, then the question is what was this one language before the time of the Tower of Babel? Traditionally it was believed to be Hebrew or a pre-Hebrew language. This belief was so revered that even in colonial American the first doctoral dissertation at Harvard College was entitled, *Hebrew as The Mother Tongue* [4]

There seems to be some linguistical validity to this idea that the first language of mankind was at least Semitic in origin. For instance the word LAD (boy) is *yalad* ‏ילד‎ Both in Hebrew, in Aramaic *yld*

---

[2] The Jerusalem Post, January 2005.
[3] Genesis 11:4-9
[4] http://www.edenics.org, What is Edenics? Page 1

ילד is the word for infant and in Arabic the word for child is *walid,* each is built upon the Semitic root word spelled Lamed, Daleth לד *(L-D).* The science of Edenics now has over 23,000 such *coincidences.*[5] The science of Edenics works with a Proto-Semitic vocabulary where each root letter has the *genes* for the wide diversity of the world's words.[6]

Edenics then moves from the Semitic languages to other world languages to show these *coincidences* such as the Hebrew word for *way or path* which is *derek* דרך which is spelled Daleth ד Resh ר Kap כ *(DRK).* In Russian it is the word *doroga* which uses the consonants DRG. The G or Gimmel ג can shift to a harder C as it passes through various dialects to sound like a Kap כ (K). Thus a slight shift in sound produces a different sounding word, yet it is still based in its original word.[7] As I personally study the Semitic languages myself I will often attempt to trace a Hebrew word to its Semitic origins. I will usually trace the triliteral root word using the first two letters. For instance there are seven different words that can be rendered as *evil.* The first two letters of the triliteral root are the same. The third letter tells you what type of evil you are dealing with. For instance *ra'ah* רעה *(Resh-Ayin-Hei)* is an evil that is a consuming passion. *Ra'av (Resh-Ayin-Beth)* רעב is an evil for famine or hunger, *Ra'al* רעל *(Resh-Ayin-Lamed)* is an evil that causes one to tremble or shake in fear.[8] Many are familiar with the word Egyptian word *ra* which refers to the Egyptian sun God. This God was not considered to be benevolent and hence you have the idea of evil.

Yet, even if we conclude that the original language before the tower of Babel was Semitic in nature and indeed Hebrew, this

[5] Isaac E. Mozeson, The Origin of Speeches (Lightcatcher Books) 2006, page i
[6] Ibid, page i
[7] Ibid, page ii
[8] Davidson, Benjamin, The Analytical Hebrew and Chaldee Lexicon (Hendrickson Publishers), 2007 pages 686-688.

opens the door to some greater questions, some that are mystical in nature.

The Nature of Language

Genesis 1:3 tells us "And God said: 'Let there be light.'"[9] This creates an interesting question because we learn that God is a spirit.[10] In the Greek the word *spirit* is *pneuma* which has the idea of *wind or breath.*[11] In the Aramaic Bible (Peshitta) the word that is used is *rucha.*[12] This is identical to the Hebrew word *ruch* which is generally rendered as spirit, wind, cool air, mind or disposition.[13] In other words a spirit has no corporal being, it is something you can feel, but cannot really see. It has no form. Thus God as a Spirit would have no physical form such as lungs, a tongue or vocal cords which are necessary to form speech. So how is it that God was able to *speak* light into being? The answer may lie in the Hebrew word used for *said* which is *'amar.* There are two words in Hebrew commonly used for speaking, *'amar* and *debar. Debar* means *to speak* but in its Semitic root it has the idea of making a connection.[14] *Amar* also means to speak, but this is a speaking which is just making a declaration, an announcement. *Amar* does not actually have to be a vocalization, it could be just a thought. [15] Thus, God just simply imagined or thought about light and there was light. He just imagined and thought about grass and there was grass.[16]

---

[9] King James Version, (Thomas Nelson, Inc.) 1976, pg. 7.
[10] Ibid., John 4:24, pg.1560.
[11] Helps Word-studies, (Helps Ministries, Inc., 1987.
[12] Aramaic Pershitta New Testament, Vol. II, Janet Magiera (Light of Word Ministry) pg. 30.
[13] Davidson, pg. 678.
[14] Davidson, pg. 144.
[15] Davidson, pg. 33.
[16] KJV, pg. 7.

Still to even think we must formulated some sort of vocabulary, do we not? Animals do not think in any language. They feel things. They feel impending atmospheric and geological changes in the earth in their physical bodies. They are in tune with all the physical elements of the earth, its electrical and magnetic fields. Birds will fly intuitively straight to their winter homes thousands of miles away. Migrating whales do much the same. Salmon return to their breeding grounds to lay their eggs.[17] Animals have a language, but it is not a language of words, it is the language of the creation, it is a language of the mind, emotions and feelings. If you have a pet dog you may think he understands every word you say, but he is really watching your eyes, your body movements and listening to the tone of our voice. He can tell if you are upset or happy. If you are upset with him it does not matter whether the words coming out of your mouth say, "Bad, nasty, terrible dog," or "Beautiful, wonderful, dear dog." No matter what words you use your pet will lower his heard and whine in despair. It is not your words he hears but your heart that he feels. So too is the language of God, it is not the words we use, the language we speak to Him in, but it is the words of our heart. These are not phonical sounds filled with vowels and consonants formed from our physical vocal cords, carried by air passing through our lungs and forming certain sounds with our tongue and lips, but they are expressions of our heart.

Scientist will tell us that thought is electrical energy. An electroencephalography (EEG) is regularly used. An EEG is a test that measures and records the electrical activity of the brain. A computer records the brain's activities on a screen as wavy lines. Certain condition s, such as seizures can be seen by the changes in the normal pattern of the brain's activity.[18] Researchers today at

[17] Fitzpatrick, Sonya, The Pet Psychic, 2003, pg. i
[18] www.webmd.com/.../electronencephalogram-eeg, pg. 1

Samsung's Emerging Technology Lab are testing tablets that can be controlled by your brain by using a cap that resembles a ski hat studded with monitoring electrodes. The computer uses a binary code of 1 and 0. It is a language in itself, but it is not words, nor does a computer understand words, it only understands, on and off. Electrical impulse and no impulse. Yet science has been able to develop machines to actually read our thoughts according to this article in the New York Times. [19]

So it is not a giant leap to say that God created the world using the energy of thought. When He created man he communicated with man by the energy of thought, but when it became necessary for man to communicate with each other God provided lungs, vocal cords, a tongue and lips to form verbal sounds to express what the energy of thought was formulating.

This then brings us to the conclusion that language is merely thought processes that are expressed in a physical realm through sounds formed from a natural human body.

Writing Systems

As civilization began to develop and began to interact in forms of trade, commerce and government, it became necessary to be able to communicate in some written form. The earliest form of writing that we have been able to uncover dates back to about 2600 BC with the Sumerians.[20] However a system of expression of one's thoughts have been found in clay tablets dating back to 4100 – 3800 BC. This is shown by pictures or logographs being impressed on clay tablets with figures to represent land, grain and cattle. Eventually this lead to a syllabic writing where symbols

---

[19] Bilton, Nick, Distruptions: Brain Computer Interfaces Inch Closer to Mainstream. New York Time, April 29, 2013 page B1.
[20] Grimbly, Shona (2000). Encyclopedia of the Ancient World (Taylor&Francis), pg. 216.

were used to represent sounds rather than words.[21] Eventually a more efficient way of expressing these pictures was to use a reed that had a triangular shape at its tip as a stylus.

By pressing the reed into the clay tablet and rotating it and using its stem to create a straight line you had a series of triangles and lines. This is known as the cuneiform style of writing. In its earliest phase cuneiform was based upon pictures and symbols. These signs were eventually adopted by the East Semitic people of Mesopotamia and Akkadia who developed the first Semitic form of writing and introduced a phonetic based alphabet that was first seen with the discovery of the clay tablets in Ugarit. The Egyptians also developed a writing system based upon a series of pictures. Some were biliteral (that is two symbols) and some triliteral (three symbols). These developed into a syllabic system where the pictures represented a consonantal sound. For instance the picture of water /\/\/\/\ became the symbol for the consonantal sound of *M*.[22]

Hebrew is classified as a Semitic language which belongs to the Canaanite group of languages which are a branch of the Northwest Semitic family of languages. Hebrew became extinct as a spoken language during the Babylonian exile in the seventh century BC when the Aramaic language became the predominant international language in the region.[23] From that point on Hebrew was used as a ceremonial language until the Twentieth Century when it was revived to become the official language of the State of Modern Israel. Presently all the writings that have been preserved in Hebrew are of an alphabetic phonetic script. That is to say the twenty two letters each symbolize a phonetic sound. However, it

---

[21] Hoffman, Joel M. In the Beginning – A Short History of the Hebrew language, (New York University Press), 2004, pg. 18.

[22] www.historian.net/hxwrite.htm, History of Writing, pg. 1

[23] Ross, Allen P. Introducing Biblical Hebrew (Baker Academic), 2001, pg. 52.

will be shown in this paper that the picture symbols are embedded in the modern Hebrew script that is used today and referred to as the Square Script or the Assyrian Script as it was believed to have developed during the Assyrian captivity.

The Hebrew Writing System

Throughout the history of the Hebrew people up to the time of captivity, the Hebrew language used various scripts that were common in the Semitic regions of the Near East. The script developed alongside others in the region during the late second and first millennia BC. The most common form was closely related to the Phoenician script, which probably gave rise to the use of Alphabetic writing in Greece. Around the time of the Babylonian exile and the destruction of the first temple in 586 BC the Jews discontinued the use of the Canaanite system and adopted what is known as the Square script which is in use today.[24]

The Babylonian Talmud however, gives a different story. The square script as it is seen today in the Hebrew Torah scrolls known as Kthav Ashurith was the original Hebrew script carved into the Ten Commandments. According to the Talmud and Jewish tradition the Ktav Ashurith was lost over time as the people began to use the script of other cultures for their day to day writing.[25]

As indicated the most common form of the Hebrew script was closely related to the Phoenician script. The Hebrews took the Phoenician consonantal system and doubled up three of the letters (Hei-h, Vav-w, and Yod-y) for use as vowels. Thus the Hei ה (h) represented not only the consonant Hei-*h* but also the vowel *a*. This made it possible to record some vowel sounds alongside the consonantal sounds. This made it possible for the first time

---

[24] Jewish Encyclopedia, Vol. I Alphabet Hebrew
[25] Babylonian Talmud, Tractate Shabbat, 104 a and Tractate Megilla 2b. and Sanhedrin 21b-22a

for non-experts to write. Writing up to this time was primarily the domain of expert scribes as it had been from the inception of writing. Only a handful of people could actually read or write. [26]

It is important to recognize that languages change and evolve over the years. The currently popular pronunciations of Hebrew, whether those of modern Hebrew or the Jewish liturgical Hebrew, reflect even the most recent innovations into the language and differ significantly from the Hebrew of 1000 years ago which reflect the oldest copy of the Hebrew Bible, let alone the Hebrew of ancient times.[27]

So in a discussion of the esoteric structure of the Hebrew Alphabet, we must remember that for the vast majority of people Hebrew was not a language that was read or written up until the time of the exile except by a few elite scribes. When I discuss the ancient meanings behind the Hebrew letters I will be speaking more of a phonetic sound than an actual picture of the letter.

It will be my theory that up to the time of the captivity that when religious teachers taught their children about God they used tonal phonetic sounds, to describe God's relationship to man and man's relationship to God. Teaching was done by oral tradition and not by reading from a text. Thus the teachers would read the Torah by memory and emphasize certain phonetic sounds. There were twenty two tonalities, two as silent, that the teachers used to express God's relationship with us and our relationship with God. These sounds were associated with letters that formed words and the teachers would stress these sounds to illustrate and emphasize their main teaching points.

During the time of captivity many Jews actually prospered and became wealthy. The Babylonian policy allowed the Jews to settle in towns and villages along the Chebar River which was

[26] Hoffman, pg. 5.
[27] Ibid. pg. 8

an irrigation channel. The Jews were allowed to live together in communities. They were even allowed to farm and perform other sorts of labor to earn an income. The prophet Jeremiah even encouraged the Jews in captivity to take wives, build houses, plant gardens and take advantage of the situation.[28]

Scripture seems to suggest that to keep their hope alive and not be assimilated into the Babylonian way of life and to preserve their identity, the religious leaders copied the Scriptures. They also wrote much literature and taught the people to observe the laws.[29]

Few have offered a definitive reason as to why the Hebrews abandoned the old Canaanite/Phoenician script for a newer Square Script. I would suggest that one reason would be that people were becoming more literate during the captivity period as they were taking on roles as merchants and business managers for the Babylonians. Many were even allowed to serve in the Babylonian government. It is very possible that a far greater number of Jews were now becoming literate and familiar with a writing system. It would follow that all the teachers of their religious leaders using tonal and phonetic expressions to illustrate and emphasize our relationship with God began to take on an actual picture with the Canaanite/Phoenician script. Yet much of this script was based upon pagan beliefs. For instance the first letter of the Alphabet was the Aleph which was pictured as an ox head.[30] In ancient times the ox and bull were considered the same animal. The ox head symbol for the Aleph more than likely originated from the pagan god Ptah which was represented as a bull. The bull was common among many Near Eastern cults and

---

[28] Hooker, Richard, Washington State University, The Hebrews, A learning Module.
[29] Ibid.
[30] Benner, Jeff A. Ancient Hebrew Lexicon (Virtual Book Worm Publishing), Ancient Hebrew Alphabet Chart, 2005.

took on various names such as Apis in Egypt and El among the Hittites.[31] The last letter of the Hebrew Alphabet is the Taw ת. The Taw ת was pictured in the Phoenician/Canaanite script as a cross or a **t**. This was the common symbol used by the goddess Tanit.[32]

If there was a real effort to maintain the Jewish identity while in captivity as well as preserve the purity of the tonal sounds as illustrations of our spiritual nature, it would stand to reason that Ezra, who was the chief scribe during the captivity period, would have been aghast to find teachers holding up a picture of an ox head or bulls head and explain that this is their forefathers concept of god as the Aleph represented God. Then to hold up the symbol of the goddess Tanit for the letter Taw and explain this as the representation of truth would have greatly disturbed Ezra to the point that he and his scribes would institute a new script for the Alphabet, designing each letter to give a more realistic picture of God's relationship to man and man's relationship to God, following the teachings of their fathers.

As an example Rabbi Michael Skobac explains that the letter Aleph א is really made up of two other Hebrew letters, the Yod י and the Vav ו. You will notice that the right upper corner of the Aleph א appears to be a Yod י, the diagonal line would be a Vav ו and the mark on the lower left hand corner would be another Yod י spelling out Yod י – Vav ו - Yod י which is one of the Hebraic names for God יוי. Thus, Ezra changed the ox head Aleph to a letter which spelled the name of God as that was the representation that the letter Aleph א was depicted by their fathers.[33]

The question does remain, did Ezra and his scribes develop this new script themselves, did they borrow it from another script

[31] Wyatt, Nicolas, Religious Texts from Ugarit, The Biblical Seminar 53 (2nd ed) (Continuum International Publishing Group) pg. 43.

[32] Tate, Karen, Sacred Places of Goddess (CCC Publishing) 2008, pg. 137.

[33] Skobac, Michael, Rabbi www.jewsforjudaism.ca, Daniel 9 The Truth of Daniel's 70 Weeks.

in common use or did they actually discover a script that was in use dating back to the time of the Exodus and was somehow lost? There is no definitive answer to that question. Joel Hoffman in his book, *In the Beginning* sets forth three theories in which we come to understand the world. The first he calls the *Dumb-Luck Theory.* This is the theory that explains everything as being coincidence. If you shuffle a deck of cards long enough it will eventually turn out that the cards are arranged in order of suit. The sun may or may not rise tomorrow, if it does it is happenstance.

Then you have the *God Theory* that explains everything as being determined by God. If you shuffle a deck of playing cards and the cards end up in order of suit then this was God's will. Finally you have the Science Theory that claims that there is an underlying order to the universe that we as humans can understand. If you shuffle a deck of playing cards and they end up arranged by suit in ascending order, then there must be some ordering force at work, like cheating. We also fully expect the sun to rise because we can know why it will rise. Many accounts of Hebrew throughout antiquity suffered from a confusion among these three theories.[34]

Hoffman chose to use the *Science Theory* for the purposes of his book. For the purposes of my paper I am choosing a slightly modified God Theory. My theory is that God knew that the Hebrew language would change over time and eventually become a dead language. He also knew that when the language was revived it would be greatly modified and when put into a modern context we would find difficulty in determining the intended meaning behind words and verses in the Bible. Thus, he allowed the Jewish teachers, sages and rabbis from the time of Moses to the time of captivity to teach the Torah using the tonal sounds as an illustration to give a deeper meaning to the words of Torah. In

---

[34] Hoffman, pg. 8-9.

my *God Theory* I believe God preserved this language in a way that no other language was preserved and that was to give us a built in commentary by translating words letter by letter using the ancient meanings and representations for each letter as a guide to a word's original intended use in a particular verse.

CHAPTER TWO
THE MEANINGS BEHIND THE HEBREW LETTERS

Two Views on the Meanings of Hebrew Letters

The Hebrew language has a unique structure which is unmatched by other languages. In other languages words represent agreed-upon conventions that attach no special meaning to the letters. In Hebrew each letter has a unique meaning which is conferred upon the word which is involved in the buildup of the word's meaning.[35]

Take for example the word for worship in Hebrew which is שחה (shachah). Hebrew is read from right to left so the first letter of the word is Shin – שׁ which has traditionally carried the meaning of passion, fire, or a fiery passion.[36] Thus worship involves a fiery passion between God and man. The second letter is Chet ח which represents a joining with God in a secret special place or a bridal chamber.[37]

[35] Shore, Haim, Coincidences in the Bible and in Biblical Hebrew (IUniverse, Inc), 2005 pg. 1
[36] Seidman, Richard, The Oracle of Kabbalah (St. Martin's Press), 2001, Pg.152.
[37] Haralick, Robert, The Inner Meaning of the Hebrew Letters (Jason Aronson, Inc.) 1995, pg. 124.

The final letter in the word שחה (shachah) is the Hei ה which represents the divine presence or the presence of God.[38] Thus, you have a built in commentary on the word for worship or שחה (shachah) which tells you that when you worship you are sharing a fiery passion with God and He with you through a joining with Him in a secret place, like a bridal chamber to experience His presence. In fact when I was in seminary I translated a poem from a Ugaritic text where the word *SK* which is the identical root word for the Hebrew word *shachah* which was used to show a sexual union between the goddess Anat and a mortal man. We learn from this built in commentary that we worship God when we enter into an intimacy with Him.

Note how the Shin ש appears like a flame of fire, hence you have the idea of a fire. Passion is often referred to as a fire. In fact in the word for fire which is אש (esh) you find the Shin appears next to the Aleph which represents God.[39] The Chet ח unlike the Hei ה is closed on the top right and left of the letter where Hei ה has an opening on the left top of the letter. The Chet ח pictures an enclosure. It is believed by esoteric rabbis that the Hei was attached to the Holy Ark that preceded the Israelites on their travels through the wilderness, because the sages teach that the cloud that enveloped them was shaped like a Hei ה thus representing the presence of God.[40]

We could take the Hoffman's *Dumb Luck Theory* and just say these are coincidences that happened randomly, or we could take his *Science Theory* that this, as well as thousands of others similar connections between a word and its letters, were a design of men or we could take the *God Theory* that this was God's Design for a language that He knew would encompass His Word.

---

[38] Scherman, Nosson/Zlotowitz, Meir, Rabbis; The Wisdom in the Hebrew Alphabet (Mesorah Publications, LTD), 1988, pg.88.
[39] Seidman, pg. 152.
[40] Scherman, pg. 88.

Even if we took two of the three theories, the *God Theory* or the *Science Theory* we are faced with the fact that the traditional meanings behind the Hebrew letters do shed light on the ancient understanding of what a particular Hebrew word was intended to mean. Based upon the *God Theory* we would have to speculate that this would be a logical thing for an infinite God, the creator of the universe to do in His book that we call the Bible. One could only imagine the wealth of knowledge and wisdom that this omniscient God could convey to mankind and to do it in just a book of a few hundred pages does not seem logical. As a Hebrew teacher I find many Christians who really seek the Lord with all their hearts, souls and might long to study the Word of God in the original languages hoping to glean more than just a surface reading of the Bible.

They have a sense that there is more to the Bible than just a surface reading. They feel there must be a reason for all the numbers in the Bible, the details in the construction of the tabernacle and the Holy Ark and even the specific design of the ark of Noah, than just to fill some pages with information that seemingly has no practical or personal value to us today.

Indeed the *Zohar*, one of the Jewish mystical books declares that every sentence, every phrase, every word, and even every letter of the Bible exists simultaneously on several levels of meaning. The Zohar declares, "Woe unto those who see in the Law nothing but simple narratives and ordinary words!...Every word of the Law contains an elevated sense and a sublime mystery."[41]

The Bible teaches us, "And ye shall seek me, and find [me], when ye shall search for me with all your heart."[42] Where can we really search and seek God but in His Word, the Bible. Yet, how do we read the Bible? Do we read it like a novel, a reference

---

[41] Hoffman, Edward, The Hebrew Alphabet (Chronicle Books), 1998, pg. 13.
[42] Jeremiah 29:13, KJV

book or even as a mystery book? Perhaps we should consider the ancient works of Judaism. The Jews do believe in the same God as Christian do. In fact the first Christians were Jewish, Jesus was Jewish and the Old Testament is a book about the Jews. Our roots, heritage and very origins as Christians lie in Judaism. Judaism is twice as old as Christianity, perhaps their identity as the *chosen people* is that they were chosen by God to lead the world into a knowledge and understanding of God.

Taking a look at Jewish tradition we find one tradition that is seemingly overlooked by Christians. Rabbi Akiva lived during the time of the Jewish rebellion against the Romans in 136 AD. According to this tradition, each letter in the Hebrew Alphabet carries a certain meaning, and indeed the true meaning of any Hebrew word can be contrived from the total sum of the meanings of the root constituent letters. The very position of the letter in the root affects the weight it contributes to the word meaning.[43]

So based upon this we could take the word for *sin* which is the same root word for *miss* חטא (chatah). We must assume that there is a relationship between these two expressions (sin and miss the mark) as they share the same root and in fact carry a certain message. In this case the relationship is simple, sin is missing the target or the mark. Paul alludes to this when he says, "I press toward the *mark* for the prize of the high calling of God in Christ Jesus."[44] Thus two words with the same root appear to be compatible in this case and are even explained by it. It also attests to the possible design in the composition of Hebrew words.[45] This, of course, is just one example and one example can be considered a coincidence. However, when examined over a wide variety of other Hebrew words using the same procedure and finding a relationship, this gives some basis to considering a purposeful design.

[43] Shore, pg. 5.
[44] Philippians 3:14, KJV.
[45] Shore, pg. 5.

This leaves us with the question as to where these meaning behind the letters originated and who originated them. There are two theories as to the origin of these meanings. One is mystical and the other in natural.

The Hebrew language is comprised of twenty-two letters, five of which are known as double (or mother) letters as they carry two distinct forms. One form is used at the beginning of a word and in the middle of a word and the second form is found only at the end of a word. Originally Hebrew was written with no space between words and one found it difficult to determine where a word begins and where one end. The final or second form of a mother letter would be used to show where a word ends. These letters are the Kap ךכ, Mem םמ, Nun ן, Pei ףפ and Tsadi ץצ. According to the mystical view these letters were known only by the righteous such as Abraham, and later Moses, Joshua and the seventy elders of Israel under their leadership. They brought the knowledge of these special letters to the Holy Land, where through the Prophets, the entire Jewish people came to use them.[46]

The *Midrash,* a Jewish commentary, venerated the Hebrew letters. They even deemed it as the language of angels and early rabbis even regarded the letters as existing independently in a transcendent realm beyond the physical world and time. They taught that when Moses received the Torah he even saw God designing crowns for the individual letters.[47] The Talmud even teaches that Bezalel built the Tabernacle in the wilderness[48] because he "knew how to combine the letters with which heaven and earth were created."[49] Thus there is the mystical belief that these letters existed before creation and indeed were the source and energy of creation

---

[46] Hoffman, pg.10
[47] Ibid.
[48] Exodus 31:1-6.
[49] Babylonian Talmud, Bavi. Tractate Beracht P. 55b.

The *Sepher Yetzirah* or *The Book of Formations* attributed to Abraham teaches that the foundation of all things is based upon the twenty-two letters and the combinations of these letters. These letters existed 2,000 years before creation[50] What is being said is that the twenty two letters are, in effect, the raw material of creation. The letters were used as an agency of creation. The letters can be ordered in countless combinations by changing their order within words and each rearrangement of the same letters results in a blend of the cosmic spiritual forces represented by the letters. To illustrate, one combination of hydrogen and oxygen produces water, while another combination produces hydrogen peroxide. So it is was with the utterances of God at creation he used different combinations of the twenty two different Hebrew letters for everything he created and these were formulated into words or a language for man so that he could communicate on a natural level.[51]

It is here that we walk a fine line into mysticism. Is there really some energy or power inherit in the letter themselves? This may not seem to be an important issue, but it can lead to an obsession to pronouncing every word correctly as a mispronunciation would not create the intended energy of the letter or word and thus it would not be put to its proper use. I am continually be confronted by people who feel that I am not moving properly in my faith because I use the word *Jesus* and not *Yeshuah* יֵשׁוּ or I used the word *God* and not *YHWH* יהוה. Yet to emphasize this would be saying that I then must pray my prayers in the Hebrew language and speak the words precisely because they are composed of Hebrew letters. Thus, I would be suggesting that by making a regular practice of speaking Hebrew I would have a special place in the afterlife. To me this would take the personal aspect

---

[50] Westcott, Wynn, translated from the Hebrew, Sepher Yetzirah or The Book of Creation, third edition, Wescott translation, pg 13.
[51] Scherman, pg. 19.

of my relationship with God totally out of context and put it into a more legalistic context than in a context of a relationship. Thus, I would prefer to avoid the mystical element associated with the Hebrew letters and move to a more moderate position and that is that the letters are merely tools to guide us into a deeper understanding of the Word of God, but there is no real power or energy associate with the letters themselves.

This then moves our use of the meanings behind the Hebrew letters from being a mystical tool to a linguistical or natural tool. This is my preferred position that the Hebrew letters are a linguistical and natural tool used to help determine the origin and intended meaning of a word. This creates another question. Are these meanings behind Hebrew letters the creation of man or God. If they are of God then we must assume they are just as inspired as the Bible. If they are the creation of man, then they are subject to error.

Jesus made some reference to the Hebrew letters when He said that not one jot or one tittle shall in no wise pass from the law.[52] There is considerable debate over just what a jot and tittle really is but it is generally agreed that they represent letters. Jesus also said, "Enter ye in at the strait gate: for wide [is] the gate, and broad [is] the way, that leadeth to destruction, and many there be which go in thereat:"[53] The Mishnah teaches that there is a narrow gate that leads to life and a wide gate that leads to destruction. The Hei ה is referred to as the broken letter. You will notice that there is a space in the upper left hand corner of the Hei ה which suggest brokenness.[54] The Hei is known as the broken letter and that space at the left hand corner is a narrow gate and the open space at the bottom of the letter is a wide gate and many fall through the wide gate but find it very difficult to climb to the narrow gate to find life.

---

[52] Matthew 5:18, KJV
[53] Matthew 7:13 KJV
[54] Haralick, pg. 79.

It is possible Jesus was making a reference to an esoteric meaning of the letter Hei.

We find in the book of Revelation, Here is wisdom. Let him that hath understanding count the number of the beast: for it is the number of a man; and his number [is] Six hundred threescore [and] six."[55] The word in the Greek for count is *psephisato* which really means to calculate. As will be explained later in this paper, every Hebrew letter has a numerical value and the sum of the numerical values of the letters comprising a given word occasionally delivers a relevant message. This is called the Gematria the process of determining the numerical value of Hebrew words to compare to other words which have the same numerical value. This is a practice of the Esoteric rabbis that was in use during the time of John when he wrote the Book of Revelation and thus he could very well have been referring and encouraging the use of an esoteric search of the Scriptures in the Hebrew language using the meanings behind the Hebrew letters as a guide.

Abraham Ben Samuel Abulafia who lived around 1240 – 1292 AD advocated a process of knowing God through the twenty-two letters of the Alphabet. He encouraged meditation on the letters by combining the letters into words from Scripture, reversing them around rapidly until one's heart feels warm. Those who adhere to this technique will receive wisdom, understanding, good counsel and knowledge....The Spirit of the Lord will rest upon them.[56] I believe what the rabbi was teaching is that we are to take a passage of Scripture, look at the words in Hebrew and make esoteric applications to these words using the Gematria and meanings behind the letters. This is a process of meditation on the Word of God and allowing the Spirit of God to reveal His truth to you. There is a benefit to a study of God's Word using commentaries and Bible study tools that have been created by man, but these

[55] Revelation 13:18
[56] Hoffman, pg. 15.

men had no more of the Spirit of God inside of them than you have, they simply had a wider experience of human knowledge. Yet it seems the rabbis of old have also encouraged us to study the Word of God in a personal way, in a way that we can allow the Spirit of God to *rest* upon us as Rabbi Abulafia encouraged.

Now all this does not suggest that the meanings behind these letters are inspired, but they are tools of man no different than our commentaries and Bible Study helps that we use. The only difference is that these tools follow about three thousand five hundred years of tradition and God may very well have guided men in the development of the Hebrew language to incorporate this hidden commentary.

The Nature of the Esoteric Structure of the Hebrew Alphabet

Of course the first question I must address is just what do I mean by esoteric structure of the Hebrew Alphabet. The word *esoteric* means "Understood by or meant for only the select few who have special knowledge or interest."[57] There is the example of poetry which is full of *esoteric* allusions. This is oppose to the *exoteric* which means to be suitable for or communicated to the general public.[58] When a physician speaks to another physician he may say something like, "This patient has suffered an acute, inferior, myocardial infarction." Speaking to a layman, like myself, he may simply say, "The patient suffered a heart attack." When physicians speak to each other the will use *esoteric* language as the physician will have a greater background of medical terminology than someone like me who has never studied medicine. The military may make a statement to the press using esoteric language to soften an otherwise emotionally charged situation. They may say

[57] Dictionary.com. Esoteric.
[58] Ibid., Exoteric

something like, "The aircraft suffered an undesirable surface to air interface" (it crashed), or "We suffered some collateral damage" (civilians were killed).

Jesus spoke esoterically by using parables to those it was granted to know the mysteries of the kingdom but to those who would not know they would then not understand his parables or his esoteric teaching.[59]

The use of esoteric language is not uncommon among Christians, we use terms not understood by others all the time such as *born again, regeneration, atonement* and many other words which have specific meaning to a Christian and yet may mean something entirely different to other groups even within the Christian community. The use of the meanings of the letters is not esoteric in the sense that only a select few are allowed to understand their meanings, but only a few really care to take the time to learn these meanings and apply them and as a result they would not understand the conclusions that someone using the meanings behind the letters would reach.

I will often quote Psalms 23:1, "The Lord is my consuming passion, I shall not want." Someone will respond and say, "My Bible says that the Lord is my Shepherd, how can you say consuming passion." I will then say that the Hebrew word for *shepherd* is רעה (ra'ah). They will then look up the word in the Strong's Concordance or their Lexicon and say, "My books do not say this, it only say it means evil, and shepherd." I will then say, "Look at this word *ra'ah* esoterically. What is the relationship between evil and shepherd." As you examine the word esoterically you discover that this particular evil is an evil of consumption or a consuming passion. A consuming passion can be bad, but it can also be good. A drug or an alcohol addiction is evil, but for a shepherd to have consuming passion for his sheep, that would be good as that would make him a good shepherd. So looking at this

---

[59] Matthew 13:11, KJV

verse esoterically, I would say, "The Lord is my consuming passion and if I am consumed with this passion for God, I will not want anything else."

Now someone who does not understand that I am simply applying my understanding of the esoteric structure of the Hebrew language would say that I am reading into Scripture, I am changing Scripture, I am even perverting Scripture. Yet, I am studying Scripture simply as the Jewish rabbis have studied it for centuries and as Jesus encouraged and demonstrated when He spoke in parables.

I need to now spell out just what is the nature of the esoteric structure of the Hebrew Alphabet.

Letters and Their Meanings

Probably the most common use of the esoteric structure is with Hebrew letters and their meanings. How do we know what each letter stands for?

Probably one of the greatest ancient sages to address this issue is Rabbi Akiva who died in 136 AD. It is traditionally believed that he produced numerous interpretations based upon the Hebrew letters. One of the most ancient Jewish documents on the Hebrew letters is the *Midrash D'Rabbi Akiva (Commentary of Rabbi Akiva).*[60] However, he drew much of his material from another source and that was the from the Gemara which is part of Jewish Talmud.[61] The Talmud is a work of thousands of Jewish scholars, sages and rabbis. There have been other modern Jewish scholars such a Elias Lipiner[62] who researched the Talmud and other ancient Jewish literature to tabulate the various mean-

---

[60] http://www.ou.org/about/judaism/rabbis/rakiva.htm
[61] Babylonian Talmud, Masechet Sahabbat (Daf 104, 1)
[62] Lipiner, Elias, The Metaphysics of the Hebrew Alphabet, 2003.

ings behind Hebrew letters as used by the sages throughout the centuries.

According to Jewish tradition the meanings behind Hebrew letters may be studied from four sources:

1. The letter name;[63]
2. The meaning of the word in the Bible, where the letter makes its first appearance as the first letter in the word (This excludes the prefix).[64]
3. The letter's geometrical shape.[65]
4. The letter's numerical value or the Gematria[66]

Let's use the example of the Aleph א which is the first letter of the Alphabet. It is also the *number one* in Hebrew (Hebrew letters are also used for the numbering system). The first appearance of the Aleph is in the word Elohim אלהם. Thus given its ordinal position God comes first and is therefore number one. It also expresses the oneness of God. The structure of the Aleph a or its geometrical shape also indicates its meaning. As indicated earlier the Aleph א is seen with two Yods which have a numerical value of 10 and a Vav which has a numerical value of 6. 10+10+6=26. Now look at the name of God יהוה YHWH. The Yod has a value of 10, the Hei has a value of 5 and the Vav has a value of 6. Thus the numerical value of God's name, YHWH is 10+5+6+5=26.[67]

Now let me do something of a Christian nature here to show that this is just not a Jewish thing. Let's look at the word Aleph אלף which is spelled Aleph-Lamed-Pei. Aleph has a numerical value of 1, the Lamed has a value of 30 and the Pei has a value of

[63] Shore, pg. 13.
[64] Babylonian Talmud, Gemara, Masechet Babba Kamma, Daf 55, 71.
[65] Shore, pg. 13.
[66] Blech, pg. xi-xiii
[67] Shore, pg. 14.

80. 1+30+80=111. One Father, One Son, One Holy Spirit. Am I stretching things, is it just a coincidence? Perhaps.

So now let us take each of the four sources one at a time.

The Letter's Name.

Each letter of the Hebrew Alphabet is also a word with its own meaning and hence contributes to the meaning behind the letter. Below is a chart showing the Letter and its word meaning. I have taken these definitions from various sources including the Lexicon, Talmud and scholarly papers. These definitions are not exhaustive, each word has wide range of meanings and I am only giving you two or three meanings for illustrative purposes. But note that all definitions are in some way related to each other.

Aleph אלה - Leadership, family, friend.[68]

Beth ב׳ת - Home, place of the heart, blessing,[69]

Gimmel גמל - Camel, to load on, to do good.[70]

Daleth דלת - Door, portal, gateway.[71]

Hei הא - Behold, I am here, power of being.[72]

Vav ואו - Nail, connection, unification.[73]

Zayin ז׳ן - Weapons, defense, sustenance.[74]

Cheth ח׳ת - Animal, mind, desires.[75]

---

[68] Davidson, pg. 30

[69] Ibid., pg. 82.

[70] Babylonian Talmud, Seder Moed Vol1, Shabbat (104a) (Soncino Press), 1938, pg. 500.

[71] Haralick, pg. 57

[72] Ginsburgh, Yitzchak, Rabbi, The Hebrew Letters (Gal Einai Publications), 1992, pg. 80.

[73] Rashi, Pentateuch and Rashi's Commentary, Genesis Vol. 1 (S.S. & R. Publishing), 1976 pg. 94.

[74] Scherman, pg. 107.

[75] Zalman, Shneur, Rabbi, Likkutei Amarim – Tanya (Kehot Publication Society), 1993, pg. 25.

Teth ט'ת - Agreeable, fasting, removing.[76]

Yod י'ו - Hand, power, portion.[77]

Kap כפ - Palm of the hand, spoon, sole of the foot.[78]

Lamed למד - To learn, teach, to prod like cattle.[79]

Mem מם - From, before, toward[80]

Nun נון - To endure, continue,[81] fish, flourish[82]

Samek סמך - To support, rely on, trust in[83]

Ayin עין - Eye, appearance, sparkle[84]

Pei פא - Mouth, speech[85]

Tzadi צד - To turn aside, against[86]

Qof קוף - Growth and holiness[87]

Resh ר'ש - Poverty, moral emptiness, beginning[88]

Shin ש'ן - Tooth, jaw[89]

Taw - ת ו - Mark, sign, line[90]

Where the Letter Makes its First Appearance

The Talmud teachers that "if you have learned much Torah, take not credit for yourself, for this is the reason you were created."[91] This is an interesting thought. We were created for God, or His

---

[76] Davidson, pg. 283.

[77] Haralick, pg. 141.

[78] Scherman, pg. 135.

[79] Seidman, pg. 91.

[80] Davidson, pg. 460

[81] Ben Nachman, Moshe, Rabbi, Ramban Commentary on the Torah, Exodus (Shilo Publishing House), 1971, pg. 579.

[82] Davidson, pg. 540.

[83] Babylonian Talmud, pg. 500.

[84] Haralick, pg. 229.

[85] Scherman, pg. 180.

[86] Davidson, pg. 640.

[87] Haralick, pg. 269.

[88] Seidman, pg. 145.

[89] Haralick, pg. 295.

[90] Ibid., pg. 309.

[91] Babylonian Talmud, Avaot 2:9

pleasure and His Word is the primary source. Man would and has done extensive research on the Word of God, particularly within Judaism. There are collections of writings that span over 2,000 years in many different and ancient languages which are still very hard to decipher. It would be impossible to go into all the studies that have been made just on one letter and even on the use of the one letter's first appearance in the Bible. As this paper is only concerned with offering the study of the Hebrew letters as a viable tool in personal Bible study, I will just highlight one letter and offer a some thoughts as to its first use in Scripture.

The classical example of the first use of a letter as a means to discover the meaning behind a Hebrew letter is with the first letter in the Bible, the letter Beth ב in the word bereshit בראשית which we commonly render as *In the beginning.* The question the sages asked is why does the Torah start with the second letter of the Alphabet and not the first letter Aleph א which represents God. Logically the Bible should start out with God. Unknown to most Christians, this questions has plagued Jewish sages, rabbis and teachers for thousands of years and even up to today. Michael J. Alter recently published an entire book addressing this question.[92] It is believed by ancient Jewish scholars that by studying the Torah, the means by which creation came into reality can be determined. By understanding how the physical world came into being man can comprehend the purpose of his creation. Since the Torah is the *blueprint* of God's creation and God's operator's manual it is necessary to understand the essential component of this manual and that is the Hebrew Alphabet. The natural starting point would be the first letter used in the Torah and that is the letter Beth or as some write it Beit.[93]

---

[92] Alter, Michael J. Why the Torah Begins with the Letter Beit (Jason Aronson, Inc.) 1998.

[93] Ibid., xxi-xxii.

One explanation that is given by the sages is that the first word in the Torah, *bereshit* of which the Beth is the commencing letter, expressing the principle of the oneness of God, the very basis of our faith both in Christianity and Judaism.[94] In Christianity we believe in one God but in three persons. Without the beth this could not be expressed. The numerical value of the word *bereshit* or BYASYT when using the *mispar katan* (digit sum) you have ב = 2, ר = 200, ש = 1, ת = 300, ' = 10 and את = 400 for a total of 913. When you add 9+1+3 you have 13. Appling the principles of the Gematria you would look at the Hebrew word *echad* אחד and find that the numerical value of that word is א = 1, ח = 8, ד = 4 which totals 13.[95] The word *echad* is the word for one and expresses the idea of oneness. Thus the Bible starts off expressing not just God but that God is one. But the Gematria would not work if the Bible started with an Aleph but starting with the Beth we have Scripture not only starting off with God but the oneness of God.

I should point out that this is even important from a Christian perspective as the word *echad* does not expresse one but expresses a unity of one, a joining together into one,[96] like ten ball players are one team. God is one, but one in an *echad* or a unity of one in three persons. Hence the Beth has taken on the meaning of a unity and you have the Beth representing a home. A home consists of a family living in unity. So the first appearance of the letter Beth shows a unity and oneness with God, a unity of a family and a home.

Going back to the first source, the meaning of the word itself for Beth, you have a home. You also have a place in the heart. Is not the unity and oneness of a home the thing that makes it a place in your heart? You also have the Beth representing blessings. We speak of many blessings but the Beth, which is the commencing

---

[94] Ibid., pg. 39.
[95] Ibid., pg. 40.
[96] Davidson, pg. 17.

or first letter in the Hebrew word for blessing *barak* ברכ teaches us that all our blessings come from one source and that is God.

The Letter's Geometrical Shape

Our third source of information leading to an understanding of the meaning behind a Hebrew letter is the very shape of the letter itself. This is where the use of the so called ancient Hebrew script, which I have shown earlier, is really a form of the ancient Phoenician script or Canaanite script and would not be used as a source to lead us to an understanding of how a Hebrew word shows us a relationship with God and God's relationship with us. For one thing, as earlier indicated, these pictures or shapes have a pagan origin and like Ezra, I am very uncomfortable with using the picture of an old Semitic god describe my relationship with God Jehovah. I also believe that this is why Ezra and his scribes either developed or reintroduced the Square script or the Assyrian script that is in use today. I believe Ezra saw the value of the meanings behind the Hebrew letters and he wanted to maintain the purity of these meanings so he either reintroduced the square script or developed a new script which would actually describe the meanings of these letters.

As I indicated earlier the ancient teachers would teach the Torah orally, very few people other than an elite group of scribes could actually read, let alone write the Hebrew. So the teachers all taught the Torah or the laws of God orally. They would use certain phonetic sounds, twenty two such sounds giving each sound a meaning to describe God's relationship with man and man's relationship with God as they would teach and quote the Torah. These phonetic sounds would be used to describe something of the nature of God our relationship to Him.

As an example we have the letter Hei ה which makes a sort of breath sound. It is similar to our letter H. The Talmud teaches that Moses was *thick of tongue* כבד לשון[97] and that he could not pronounce any of the names of God because he needed to use his tongue, so God gave him a name which he could speak without using his tongue, he would speak this name of God with his breath. That name was YHWH יהוה, He would speak the name with the very breath of his life. The sages would teach that man became a living being by the breath of God, the sound of the Hei ה and then he would breathe out the letter Hei ה to illustrate.[98]

As mentioned earlier when the people of Israel entered into captivity by the Assyrians and later the Babylonians, they acquired vocations in commerce and industry where it became necessary to learn to read and write. The Hebrew language of the Israelites soon gave way to the Aramaic language and as the people of Israel were becoming literate they began to associate these phonetic sounds used by their teachers with the Canaanite Alphabet that was used for the Aramaic language at that time.

There are three possible reasons why the square script as used in Hebrew today was adopted for the Hebrew language. One reason would be the common reason that is given and that is that the language and script just evolved into the square script. I have rejected this for the following reasons. I have examined the many different scripts used in the Ancient Near East. There are many charts which show a comparison of the script. These charts try to show how the square script was a natural result of the evolutionary process of the changing script. However, like evolution, there are many missing links that would account for a sudden jump in the form of many letters.

---

[97] Elliger, K. Rudolph, W. Biblica Hebraica Stuttgartensia, Exodus 4:10, (Deutsche Bielgesellschaft), 1975, pg. 91.
[98] Genesis 3-4, KJV.

For instance a pictograph by Jeff Brenner gives a chart showing the development of the Hebrew script from Early (Paleo) to Middle (Canaanite) to Late (Square Script). For the Aleph he shows the picture of an ox head or bulls head. The Early Aleph then become a triangle with the one line going through the middle giving the idea of horns for the Middle Aleph and then a major jump to the Aleph א as we know it today in the square script. The Beth in the Early script looks like a square script Teth and a Pei in the Middle script resembles the form of the Beth in the Square Script ב.[99]

One can easily see the similarities between the Early and Middle script but the jump to the Late script (Square Script) is just too fantastic. It is like in evolution finding the link that makes the transition from water animals to birds or land animals. The argument is to give it enough time. But in language you are only speaking of a few hundred years and that is not enough to develop and entirely different script.

The second reason for the use of the square script would be the one given by Jewish mystics. This is to say that the Square Script was really developed by God two thousand years before creation and it was the script used on the Tablets where the Ten Commandments were written. Because of the sin of the people the original script was lost.[100] Some ancient writers would give a more natural reason for the script being lost in that the people started intermixing with other races and nations and were not concerned with keeping their identity as God commanded. As a result they adopted the languages and writing systems of other cultures. This is a more of a supernatural view of the script.

My position would be somewhere in the middle and that is that Ezra and his scribes saw the people of Israel were becoming more literate and more assimilated into foreign cultures. Realizing

---

[99] Brenner, Ancient Hebrew Chart.
[100] Babylonian Talmud, Tractat Shabbat, 104a

that the Hebrew language was dying they wanted to preserve it to be at least a ceremonial language as well as one that used a script which did not allude to foreign or pagan gods and culture. Thus Ezra and his scribes took the meanings behind each letter and developed a script which would picture the spiritual meaning behind each word. In this way they would not only preserve the purity of the language but would also give future generations a built in commentary to use when translating the Word of God into whatever language they adopted in future times. Ezra realized as any linguist today knows that once a language dies out as a common spoken language many of its nuances, colloquial and idiomatic understandings will become lost, even if they manage to preserve the basic root meaning of a word. By using these spiritual values given to each letter one can dial a combination, so to speak, on the triliteral root word and discover its original intended use and/or meaning.

Thus Ezra and his scribes developed a script, based upon the known script but with many variations to reflect the sacred meanings that had been given to these letters by their forefathers. As I indicated with the Aleph. Since the Aleph represents God they took two Yods and a Vav א and created a letter which spelled God's name.

The Gimmel ג is a picture of a person running after another who is needy in order to be of help and service. Hence it follows the meaning of loving kindness *(gamelet hasidim)* and mercy.[101] The Samek ס is the only letter that comprises two aspects. A rounded blank interior and an encompassing frame around it. The Samek is often shaped like an O. It suggest that it is a symbol of God who is entirely spiritual in nature (outer frame) without any physical form (inner empty area). Also the round closed frame alludes to the earth which is filled with the glory of God.[102]

---

[101] Hoffman, pg. 27.
[102] Scherman, pg. 160.

Each letter tells a story of what its meaning represents and each meaning represents some aspect of the nature of God and his relationship to mankind and theirs to Him. Such stories can even guide us into a physical understanding of how to represent the message of a word. For instance, take the word *hallal* הלל which is the root word for Hallelujah. The word Hallelujah means *Praise the Lord* in any language. The question that can be asked is, "How do we praise the Lord, is there some physical manifestation in our praise?" The picture given by the word itself would answer that question. The word is spelled Hei, ה followed by two Lameds לל. As indicated earlier the Hei ה represents breathe and the presence of God. God breathes upon us with His presence in praise as we use two Lameds לל. Look at the Lamed ל, that little bump in the middle of the letter represents your heart.[103] Lamed ל is the first letter in the word *lev* לב which is the word in Hebrew for heart. If you put the two Lameds לל together facing each other, those two bumps will give you the picture of a heart. It is true that the symbol of the valentine heart has its origins in the middle ages around 1400 AD.[104] But who is to say that God did not have this in mind when he prompted Ezra and his scribes to design the Lamed. Perhaps God knew that at some late time in history there would be a controversy over the raising of uplifted hands to heaven in praise and worship and God wanted to give us something from antiquity to confirm this gesture. For you see the Lamed ל is the tallest letter in the Hebrew Alphabet and the stem is reaching up to heaven as if it is a raised hand reaching up to heaven to offer something from one's heart or to receive from heaven something into their heart.[105] Thus the word for praise using the Hebrew letters gives us a picture of two uplifted hands toward heaven לל

---

[103] Ibid, pg. 139.
[104] Kemp, Martin, The Heart in Christ to Coke: How Image Becomes Icon. (Oxford University Press) 2011, pg. 81-113
[105] Seidman, pg. 91-96.

seeking to give or receive something in their hearts. Can you think of a better definition of praise?

The Ayin ע looks as if it has two eyes at the end of two stems and it is observing something. Indeed the word Ayin עין means *eye* and even sounds like the English word eye. The eye needs light to see and thus you have a meaning of the letter Ayin as light or enlightenment, insight, or knowing.[106]

The Daleth ד looks like an open door and the word Daleth means a doorway or portal.[107] In my office I have a mailbox post with a ninety degree bend. It looks like a Daleth and from it I have hung a mirror. It is the picture on the cover of my manual that I use to teach my Hebrew Word Study classes. I also have a number of stories that I am preparing to publish called *Beyond the Daleth*. These are stories of fantasy journeys I take through my mirror in an Alice in Wonderland style. I take these journeys accompanied by Hebrew letters from certain words I have been studying and then in this fantasy land behind my Daleth, the Hebrew letters teach me a deeper meaning behind the Hebrew word I am studying. This is the picture of a Daleth, it is a doorway or a portal to a deeper knowledge of God.

As with the Aleph, a Hebrew letter may often be a combination of other Hebrew letters. For instance the Chet ח according to the Talmud is composed of two letters either two Zayins זז or two Vavs וו which are connected by a roof. It is a picture of a joining together of man and God.[108]

The Teth ט shows a little jot pointing toward the center of the letter as if indicating one should examine oneself. The Teth is a picture of judging and peering into the depths of oneself.[109] The letter Teth is the first letter in the word *Tov* טוב. Tov means good, but a sincere, real

---

[106] Ibid, pg. 118-124.
[107] Hoffman, pg. 30-31.
[108] Babylonian Talmud, Shabbath 104b.
[109] Haralick, pg. 130-131.

good not a false good, thus there must be closer inner examination to really achieve *Tov* or good.

The Pei פ visually resembles a mouth with a tooth. The picture displays the meaning of the word as a letter which expresses speech. Speech affects us not only physically but emotionally and spiritually. The Pei encourages us to be careful with our speech.[110]

The Resh ר is a letter that is bent over. The Talmud teaches that it is bent over because it cannot bear to look at the wicked ones. It represents a turning away from wickedness, a repentance, a change of course or direction.[111] Could Ezra and his scribes come up with any better picture for *repentance* than a bending line?

The Zayin ז carries the idea of defense, protection. The word Zayin means arms or weapons. And if you look at the Zayin, it does appear to look like a sword. The message of Zayin is that weapons are to be used only for peace, protection and defense against those who wish to destroy peace.[112]

The Vav ו is one of the few letters that retains its shape from the early Canaanite script. It is just a straight line with a little tag on top resembling a tent peg. A tent peg is used to connect the tent to the ground. The Vav in Hebrew grammar is a conjunction which connects two thoughts. It is a picture of making a connection. To the ancient Hebrew teachers it was a picture of connecting heaven to earth.[113]

The Yod ' is the smallest letter in the Hebrew Alphabet, it is the only letter that does not touch the line on the page. It sort of floats in the air. There is absolutely no similarity between the Yod in the Square Script and the Yod from the Canaanite script.[114]

---

[110] Hoffman, pg. 68-70.
[111] Babylonian Talmud, Shabbath 104b.
[112] Haralick, pg. 103.
[113] Haralick, pg. 87.
[114] Renner, Ancient Hebrew chart.

The Yod from the Canaanite script resembled an arm and later a closed hand. The Yod in the Square Script is just a little mark floating in the air. It speaks of the beginning as all matter started from a tiny point and exploded outward, it marks a beginning which is often very small and then grows. In grammar the Yod is used to indicate a future tense. The future is but a speck out there that we can barely see.[115]

The Tsade **צ** carries an idea of righteousness and humility.[116] In fact if you look that the Tsade, it will look as if someone is bowing on his knees. The shape of the Tsade tells you what the letter is all about, what its meaning really is and that is humility, righteousness, one who is continually on his knees before God seeking His guidance.

Many of these letters also carry more than one picture. For instance the Shin V is a picture of a fire burning. It is also a picture of claw or teeth in a jaw which is what the word Shin means. Fire is totally consuming. When you eat you totally consume and eliminate the refuse through urine, which is the word for another form of the letter called Sine. It has the idea of whole, entire, intact or complete. As with eating you repeat the process over and over so it also has the idea of repeating.[117]

The Kap k is another example of multiple pictures. The Kap appears like an empty cup that needs to be filled. It also looks like the palm of a hand. Both can be filled with something, both are empty. Thus you have the idea of something that is waiting to be filled.[118]

Although there may be more than one picture displayed by each letter, all these pictures still relate to each other in some way.

[115] Seidman pg. 77-83.
[116] Munk, Michael, Rabbi The Wisdom of the Hebrew Alphabet (Mesorah Publications), 1988, pg. 192.
[117] Haralick, pg. 295.
[118] Seidman, pg. 84-90

That is the nature, the beauty and the genius of the script that I believe was developed by Ezra and his scribes to maintain the purity and the original intent of the Hebrew language and the meanings behind ancient Hebrew words which have long since lost their original intent but still carry a hint of their original meaning embedded within the shapes and images of each letter.

Thus, many of the meanings that we attribute to the Hebrew letters not only come from their names, and their position in the Torah, but from the very shapes as well. We must keep in mind that all the meanings from these three sources are always somehow related as that is the nature of the Hebrew language as it is with all Semitic languages. These are relationship languages.

The Letters Numerical Value

I will be going into the Gemetria later in this book. However, I do need to address the fourth source that the ancient sages used to develop the meaning behind each letter and that is their numerical value.

The meanings of the Hebrew letters are indirectly inferred by the numerical value of a letter. Let me explain it this way. The Aleph and the Ayin are both silent letters. Why would the Alphabet have two letters that make no sound? Would not one letter be enough? One explanation is based upon the meaning of the letters. The Aleph represents God and the Ayin represents insight or enlightenment. If we use the letters to assist us in understanding an intended meaning of a specific Hebrew word then it would make sense to have two silent letters which mean two different things. For instance you have the word *ra'ah* ראה which means to see both in a physical and spiritual sense. Then you have the word *ra'ah* רעה which means evil or a consuming passion, it could also mean friend. You will note in the transliteration into the English script they read and are identical in pronunciation. Yet, these words are different in the Hebrew as the second letter in the word *to see* is an Aleph and the second letter in the word *evil* is an Ayin. Clearly, two different letters are used for two different words yet they sound the same and the differences in letters are there to indicate which word we are talking about.

However, there are two other reasons for having two letters that are silent. The Aleph represents God and the Ayin represents enlightenment or insight. If one were to examine a word and use the meanings behind the letters to arrive at some understanding of the word, then for one word you would want to include the idea of God in the word and the other you would want to include the idea of insight into the word. Thus another reason for two silent letters is to allow for the study of the word by using the meanings behind the letters.

A third reason is its numerical value. This was shown earlier with the reason for the Torah beginning with the Beth rather than the Aleph. Had the Torah began with an Aleph, the whole understanding of God and His oneness would not be shown. We would then not have a meaning for the Beth as unity of oneness.

The Value of Knowing and Using the Meanings Behind Hebrew Letters

The meanings behind these Hebrew letters are drawn from numerous sources. However all are related back to the Babylonian Talmud, Mishnah, Midrash and Gemera, which are all works dating back to the first millennium AD. Up until this time much of this information was passed down from generation to generation through oral tradition. Some information does come from the mystical books of the Kabbalah. I have studied the Kabbalah as only a reference to develop my skills with the Aramaic and not to gain any spiritual insights. However, although I do not embrace much if not all of the teachings of the Kabbalah from my limited study, I did find the references to the Hebrew letters interesting and offering a key to understanding some of the meanings behind the Hebrew letters from a non-mystical standpoint. I will need to state at this point that I do not accept any teaching that there is some form of energy or power within the Hebrew letters as taught by the Jewish mystics. However, I do believe there was a intention and purpose behind giving meanings to the letters to aid in personal study of the Bible. I personally use the meanings behind Hebrew letters for linguistical purposes only and not to gain any mystical experience.

With that being said I need to explain that I do believe there is value in considering the meaning behind Hebrew letters when you are translating the Bible for your own personal study. I am not a linguist nor am I a Bible translator, I am merely a student of ancient languages. However, as an undergraduate student and a graduate I studied under different Hebrew professors who all were actively involved in the translation work for the New International Version of the Bible. In fact my Advanced Hebrew professor in seminary was on the executive committee for the New International Version of the Bible. This committee made the final decision as to which renderings were to be included in the New International Version. I was one of two students studying under this professor who shared with us the process and problems in translating the Bible.

Also, my younger brother is a trained linguist with Wycliffe Bible Translators and spent fifteen years in Papua New Guinea translating the Bible into the Amanad language. He was also an instructor in linguistics at the Moody Bible Institute. He has given me valuable insight into the problems, difficulties and the dangers involved in translating the Bible. Based upon the insights

I received from these experiences, I am convinced that the use of the meanings behind Hebrew letters would not be an appropriate tool for Bible translators however, I do believe it would be a valuable source for an individual Christian, pastor or Christian worker in their own person study of the Bible.

The Three Keys to Translation from a Semitic Language.

Actually, linguistically, there are only two keys, to translation. The third key is the one that would be employed with the use of the meanings behind the Hebrew letters. The first key is the major and dominate key and that is the technical aspect. Under the technical aspect of translation you have to the consider factors related to grammar, syntax, exegesis, cultural input, historical information, etymologies as well as the other aspects involved in translation work.

However, when dealing with a Semitic language there is another factor that must be considered and that is to put your translation into an emotional context. Here is where we enter an area that no translator can adequately handle. For instance you have the Hebrew word libabethini לבבתני which is found in Song of Solomon 4:9. I examined nine different modern translations and found that litababethini לבבתני were all translated differently:

For the word *libabethini* לבבתני we find nine different renderings ranging from *ravished, stolen, captivated, made my heart beat faster, charmed me, taken hold, wounded, emboldened and captured.* All these words essentially mean the same thing yet each has a little different take. Each, within its emotional context offers something a little different. Here King Solomon is saying that one glance from his beloved and she has done something to his heart. Now this is important to the individual Christian as many will take this as a picture of what we do to the heart of God when we just give him a glance. For one translator we *ravish* God's heart. To us the idea of *ravishing* someone is to seize and rape. Is that what we do to God's heart? Another translator says that we have *stolen* God's heart. That gives the impression that God gives himself totally to us. Another translator says that we have *captivated* God's heart. That is less emotional and more of the idea that one glance merely gets God's attention. It could be that we make God's *heart beat faster.* This would suggest that God has a deep longing for us. Perhaps we just *charm* God's heart. He is delighted with us like we would be with a little child who smiles at us. Maybe we just *embolden* God's heart, that would mean that one glance from us and we somehow give Him the courage to approach us. A more aggressive type of response is that we have *captured* his heart. That has a much stronger emotional context than *taken hold* or *emboldened.* Captured expresses more of the idea taking by force where captivated has more of a fascination type hold on someone.

So even though all the renderings for *libabethini* are in themselves correct, they are all very different. For one thing, this is the reason the Talmud teaches that there are *seventy faces of Torah* because one word can have a wide range of meaning. This range of meaning however, is an emotional one. Depending upon one's relationship with God, one's view of God, one's experience with God and one's maturity with God will determine which word will apply.

The Douay version uses a word which is seemingly unrelated to all the other words used that is the word *wounded.* The Douay uses this word probably because the word *libabethini* is rooted in a Semitic word which means to tear bark from a tree, when you tear bark from a tree you wound that tree. Now this little insight might help us with the emotional context for what King Solomon is saying to his beloved and that is just one glance from her and she has stripped the cover off his heart making him vulnerable like a tree is vulnerable when the bark is stripped off.

Still the bottom line is that we are not going to find an adequate rendering of *libabethini* without an emotional context and for some unemotional, scientific scholar sitting up in his lofty tower, who hasn't kissed his wife in twenty years, you just have to wonder what type of emotional context he is going to translate *libabethini*. Only the one reading this passage for his own benefit will be able to find the right emotional context to put this word into.

That is why I would add a third level of translation which is not of a scientific or scholarly nature. It is not even of an academic nature. Yet, because we are dealing in the realm of the Spirit and speaking of a Book written by a supernatural God I must, for the moment, lay aside the technical and scientific level and move to a spiritual level. I would suggest that besides the technical level needed in Scriptural translation and putting a translation into its emotional context, we must consider one other factor and that is the revelatory work of the Holy Spirit. The whole idea behind the seventy faces of Torah is not that we cannot know specifically and precisely how a passage is to be rendered but that God created His Word to be read at different levels of maturity and personal character.

Our Western mindset is very technical and scientific and therefore we believe there must be just one rendering and one translation. In other words, the nine different renderings for the word *libabethini* would suggest to the Western mindset that only one is right and the rest are mistranslations. Yet, someone of an Eastern Semitic mindset would have no problem with nine different renders for they would view the Scriptures as a work of art. We, in Western culture tend to grade a painting on the skill of the artist, by his style and brush strokes. However, to truly judge a work of art we must interpret this painting by how it affected us emotionally.

We must do the same with Scripture, we would judge and grade a translation on the skill and background of the translator, but we must interpret Scripture by putting it within our own emotional context. With the revelation of the Spirit of God one can take one of the seventy faces of Torah and make a personal application in one's own private study. In this way Scripture can become something personal from a personal God. Ten years later that same passage may have an entirely different shade of meaning because one will have grown in his relationship with God and thus God can use the ambiguity of the Hebrew words to give that person a new and deeper message from the same Scripture.

With this in mind, I will present my meanings behind the Hebrew letters that I have gained from my research over the years and would encourage a Christian to use this in their own personal study and seek the guidance of the Holy Spirit to give a personal message.

The Apostle Paul instructed that we are to let the peace of God rule our hearts.[119] The word for *rule* in the Greek is *brasevet* which means to arbitrate or umpire.[120] If you are watching a baseball game and you see a player touch a base with the ball before the runner reaches the base you and everyone else knows that he is out. The umpire yells "out" but no one pays attention for they know he is out. Yet if the player touches the base with the ball the same time the runner touches the base and you have half the audience screaming "out" and the other half screaming "safe" this is when you need an umpire, to call the close ones. When using the meanings behind the Hebrew letters in your own personal

---

[119] Colossians 3:15 KJV
[120] Louw, Johannes P. Greek-English Lexicon of the New Testament (United Bible Societies), 1988.

study, you will need an umpire. Paul tells us that that umpire is the peace of God in your heart. When you find a combination of meanings that you are at peace with in your heart then this is very likely the message that God wants to give to you. For example, in the list of nine different words for *libabethini* the key to knowing which one is the correct word, is to decide on the one you feel the most peaceful with. In other words the correct rendering is the one you put into an *emotional context*.

Meaning of Each Hebrew Letter.

Aleph א

The Aleph is the first letter of the Hebrew Alphabet. As the first letter it would naturally be a reference to God. The Talmud teachers that God created the world by using the twenty two letters of the Alphabet.[121] The Zohar tells the story of the letters of the Alphabet that appeared before God to argue their case as to why they should be the letter to use in creation. Regarding the Aleph we have the account:

> The letter Aleph stood outside and did not enter. The Holy One, blessed be He, said to it, Aleph, Aleph, why do you not enter and and stand before Me like the other letters? It replied: Master of the Universe, because I saw that all the letters left You without benefaction. So what shall I do there myself? Not only that, but You have already presented the letter Beth with the greatest gift of all. And it would not be proper for the Supernal King to take back the gift, which He presented to His servant, and give it to another! The Holy One, blessed be he, said

---

[121] Babylonian Talmud, Berachot 58a

Aleph, Aleph, even though the world is created with the letter Beth, you shall be the first (lit. head) of all the letters. My attachments shall be expressed only by you and a calculations and actions of the people shall commence with you. Therefore, all unity shall be expressed by the letter Aleph.[122]

Even among the Jewish mystics the letter Aleph holds an honored place as a letter that brings all of creation into unity with God. Thus, the main focus of the letter Aleph has been one of *unity with God.* The Aleph is considered the leader and master letter of the Hebrew Alphabet. It has a numerical value of 1 and is cognate to the word Aleph אלף which means thousand.[123] But it can also mean an indefinitely large number or quantity that is innumerable, thus it carries the idea of being infinite as well. As indicated earlier the word Aleph has a numerical value of 111. Another word in Hebrew that has a numerical value of 111 is *maseveh* מסוה and means *a veil or face covering.* This word is used in the story of Moses when he had been with God and the glory of the Lord was so bright on his face that he had to put a *veil* on his face.[124] The sages teach that in the context of the Aleph א (value of 111) we can understand that the מסוה (veil = 111) means that the א has a veil and is hidden, therefore its sound is silent.[125]

There is an interesting phenomena or scribal abnormality with the Hebrew letter Aleph that is found in Leviticus 1:1. This is not seen in your standard Hebrew text, *Biblia Hebracica Stuttgartensia* that is used in Christian Bible Colleges and Seminaries because it tends to border on the suggestion that there is a significance to

---

[122] Zohar, Annotated and Explained (Skylight Illuminations), 2002, Prologue 6:38.
[123] Davidson, pg. 30.
[124] Exodus 34:33, KJV.
[125] Rashi, Pentateuch and Rashi's Commentary, Exodus Vol 2 (S.S. and R. Publishing) 1976. Exodus 34:33 pg. 438.

the Hebrew letters and their meanings. However, in your standard Jewish Hebrew Bibles the Aleph in the first words of Leviticus 1:1 וַיִּקְרָא אֶל (and he called unto) these Alephs are half the size of the Alephs that are used in the rest of the Hebrew Bible. This indicates that we must search for a rearrangement of the letters for a richer meaning.[126] I will go into further detail on this in a future chapter. However, I present this here to show that there are very subtle suggestions that Hebrew letters bear some greater significance than just to identify certain words. The Orthodox Jews believe that Moses wrote the Book of Leviticus and he deliberately shrunk the Aleph to show his humility as the Aleph represents God and Moses felt inadequate to receive a call from God with a regular size Aleph.[127] This also indicates that the Aleph carries the strongest representation of God and the oneness of God.

This oneness of God being expressed in the first letter of the Alphabet, the Aleph makes the oneness of God so fundamental to the Jewish faith that the declaration of the *Shema* is the first verse a child is taught, "Hear oh Israel the Lord our God is one."[128] It is taught to a child at his mother's knee and is the last thing a Jew utters with his final breath before departing from this world. During the long History of Jewish exile and suffering Jews have given up their lives rather than renounce their faith in God's Unity and Oneness.[129]

Even if a Jew does not give much thought to the meaning behind Hebrew letters, he cannot escape the powerful significance of the Aleph and what it means to his faith and His life. The silence of the Aleph signifies that everything each of us accomplishes, however important in daily life, first emanates from stillness and silence.[130]

---

[127] www.aish.com Weekly Torah Portion, May 21, 2009.
[128] Deuteronomy 6:4 KJV.
[129] Zalman, Tanya 2:12.
[130] Hoffman, pg. 20.

Silence is nothing and yet it is everything. The Aleph, as silent letter, expresses nothingness, and yet it is everything. Rabbi Aaron of Karlin was once asked what he had learned from his teacher, the Great Maggid. He replied that he learned nothing at all. When he was pressed to explain what he meant by that he said: "The nothing at all is what I learned, I learned the meaning of nothingness, I learned that I am nothing at all before the I AM."[131]

I earlier explained how the Aleph was formed by the letters Yod, Vav, and Yod spelling out one of the names of God. There is yet another picture of its shape and that is that the Aleph embodies ambiguity. Ambiguity is the driving of two ways. The Aleph is formed by a Yod in the upper right and a Yod in the lower left with the letter Vav lying diagonally between them.[132]

This shows how we are embracing both form and emptiness, the two dynamics of the Aleph representing God and nothingness. The Vav in the Aleph is like a ladder extending between heaven and earth. Thus, the Aleph creates the idea of God giving form to man who was originally nothing. Through Jesus Christ we move from an emptiness to a substance in the presence of God.

So the Aleph teaches us of the oneness of God, the unity of God in three persons and our unity with God. Aleph is also the first letter of the Alphabet, so it reminds us of beginnings. When we accept Jesus Christ as our Savior we enter a beginning in our relationship with God. All the letters that follow teach us what that relationship with God is like and what it entails. Aleph represents a beginning.

The Vav separating the two Yods also suggest an embracing both sides of life, the grief and the joy, the bitter and the sweet. For the Vav connects us to heaven and both sides of life have the ability to draw us closer to our creator. We can rejoice in the good

131 Seidman, pg. 16.
132 Ibid., pg. 17.

times and praise God and we can also rejoice in times of trouble[133] for it is those times that we also can draw closer to God.

Finally, the Aleph is silent and also represents God. Thus the Aleph calls us to silence before God. I once had a rabbi tell me that silence was so necessary for it is in silence that you can hear the world crying, it is in silence that you can hear the suffering of the world. In my book, *Hebrew Word Study, A Hebrew Teacher's Call to Silence,* I explain how in my week of living in silence at a trappist monastery where the brothers all took vows of silence and for one week I lived in silence my heart heard what my ears could not hear, my heart saw what my eyes could not see, and my heart spoke what my lips could not say.[134] The Aleph calls us to be silent before God who speaks to us in silence, he speaks the Words of His heart to our hearts in silence. I once attended a prayer meeting where there was this feeling that someone had to be talking the whole time. Any silence would be uncomfortable so someone had to be praying or at least saying something like "praise the Lord, bless you Lord, etc." Yet, so much can be spoken in silence. I once observed an elderly couple just sitting on a dock overlooking a lake during the sunset. They sat holding hands, looking out over the waters and saying nothing, yet they were speaking volumes to each other. Just being in each other's presence was enough to create intense communication.

Christians must learn to embrace the Aleph and learn to be silent before God. To learn to just enjoy being in the presence of God and allowing God to enjoy their own presence. We really do not need to speak words to God for God does not listen to the words of our mouth, but to the words of our heart. The two sides of the Aleph teaches us that dichotomy.

---

[133] James 1:2 KJV.

[134] Bentorah, Chaim, Hebrew Word Study A Hebrew Teacher's Call to Silence (Westbow Press), 2012. Pg. 1.

All the letters of the Hebrew Alphabet have a dark side so to speak, a warning or as the sages call it, a shadow. The shadow of the Aleph is that it lies so close to the Ultimate nothingness that it carries the danger of a belief that our existence is senseless or useless. However, if we have drifted to that extreme we must remember there are two sides to the Aleph, a direction that moves toward form and development. Another danger is that we fail to see both sides, we may become like Hamlet and will be unable to choose and act. But like Hamlet we can be aroused to action when we realize that not choosing is in itself a choice.[135]

The meaning behind the Aleph can be summed up with the following words:

Primary meaning:

1.   God
2.   Unity with God
3.   Unity of man with God
4.   Nothingness
5.   Silence before God

Shadow meaning;

1.   Ambivalence
2.   Sense of worthlessness or uselessness

Beth ‎בּ

The Beth is also the number 2, hence is speaks of duality. The Midrash states: "Why was the world created with a ‎ב? To teach you that there are two worlds." [136]The Beth reminds us that there

---

[135] Seidman, pg. 17-18.
[136] Midrash Rabbah, Genesis, Vol 1 (Soncino Press), 1983, pg. 9.

is a physical world and a supernatural world. There is a heaven and there is an earth. This duality also speaks of a duality in man, there is man and there is woman. A man and woman will make up a home. The meaning of the word for Beth comes from the root word *byith* בּיה which in itself means a home or a dwelling place. The duality of the Beth tells us that we have two homes, one on earth and one in heaven.

In the Old Testament we find over two thousand instances where some form of the word *byith* היב is used. Genesis alone has over forty five instances. The house is a place in which we live. It is the place where our essence becomes manifest.[137]

Scribes were to employ great care when writing the letter Beth. When it was written in the Ashuritic script (a special script used in writing the sacred scrolls) the Beth had to have the appearance of being composed of three connecting lines or Vavs. It was to resemble a square yet open on the left side.[138]

Other schools of thought as with the Mishnah Sofrim, declared that the Beth is composed of two letters, a Daleth and a Vav. If the Beth is too round at the top and the bottom line does not protrude out of the right, it might be confused with the letter Kap כ.[139]

As mentioned earlier the first letter of the Bible is a Beth, this was necessary to confirm the oneness of God through its numerical value. The Midrash HaGadol suggest that the Bible begins with a Beth to tell you that there is nothing before the Beth expect the Aleph, there is nothing before the world except God. [140]

---

[137] Schneerson, Menachem, Rabbi, In The Garden of the Torah (Sichos Press), 1994, pg. 2.

[138] Ginsburgh, Yitzchak, R. The Alef-Beit: Jewish Thought Revealed Through the Hebrew letters (Jason Aronson), 1991, pg. 41.

[139] Vogel, Yona, trans. Mishnas Sofrim (The Jewish Learning Exchange), 1983, pg. 26-27.

[140] Fish, Solomon, Midrash Hagadol on the Pentateuch (Manchester University Press) 1940, pg. 51.

They mystical leader of the Chasidic movement, the Baal Shem Tov suggested that the Torah started with the Beth to teach that we should not reach the Aleph (the true one God) in our understanding of it (the Aleph).[141]

Generally, the idea is that God is beyond the natural realm, we cannot fully understand God. So when he created the natural word, the Beth reminds us that we may come to understand many things in the natural world, but there are many things in the spiritual world, the world of God that we will never understand in this natural existence. Such questions as to why there is evil, why there is suffering, how can the trinity exist are things that only God will understand and we must not attempt to understand them. The Torah starts off with the Beth to remind us of what we can understand and what we can't.

As the Beth is the second letter of the Alphabet and indicates a duality, the Beth reminds us of the duality that exist on our plain of existence that took place at creation;

Day 1 - Light and Darkness
Day 2 - Waters above the sea, waters below
Day 3 - Seas and Dry lands
Day 4 - Day and Night
Day 5 - Fish swim in water, birds fly in the air
Day 6 - Animated Creatures and Spiritual man
Day 7 - Holy (Rest) from the Mundane (Creativity)

The Beth is also a preposition rendered as, *in, at, by among, with, by means of, or through.* The Beth is a house or home and we are in the house so that the house can be a means of doing something. Through it we can exercise our capabilities. One example is that the Hebrew word for *in, it* or *in her* בה shows that we can

[141] Glinert, Lewish, The Joys of Hebrew, (Oxford University Press), 1992, pg. 44.

exercise the capability of love *'ahav* אהב.[142] In other words the a for *God* who is *in* (ב) the home (ב) establishes love through the woman (ח). The Hei ח is added at the end of a word to express a feminine form of the word. Thus the Beth can represent the home which represents love and the heart.

The numerical value of the root word for Beth ב'ת is 412. Another word which has a value of 412 is *Ta'evah* אהב. This word means *desire, longing, lust, craving, delight,* or *desirable thing.* All these words are matters of the heart. The Beth represent the heart. The house is a place of the heart.

Interesting that the second word in the Bible also beg ins with a Beth, *bara'* ברא. This means to *create.* What do we know about *creation?* The word *create* can be broken into רא and ר. The רא stands for רא which means *light.* The Beth ב as we established means house and/or love. Thus creation is housed in the light and love of God (א).[143]

You will note that the Beth ר is closed on one side. The Zohar teaches that when Moses asked to see the glory of God, God only showed him His back.144 Yet God was open on the other side (like the Beth) so as to illumine the higher worlds. It is also open on one side in order to receive from the higher worlds, like a hall in which guests gather. For this reason the Beth was placed at the beginning of Torah and was later on filled in.[145] We also learn that the Beth is closed on three sides and open on the left because that is the house of the world. God is the place of the world but the world is not His place.[146]

What is being taught is that that opening on the third side is an opening to receive or be filled with the presence of God. Our

[142] Babylonian Talmud, Shabbat, 104a

[143] Glazerson, Matityahu, Rabbi, Hebrew, The Source of Languages (HaSefarim) 1988, pg. 31.

[144] Exodus 33:23 KJV.

[145] Levertoff, Paul trans. The Zohar (Soncino Press), 1978, pg. 67.

[146] Kaplan, Aryeh, Rabbi, The Bahir (Jason Aronson), 1995, pg. 6

homes are to be filled with the presence of God, this world as our home is be filled with the presence of God although this is not God's place.

During the nomadic times of the early Jews, houses were tents, temporary dwelling places. For hundreds of years Jews wandered at home in their tents, praying in their tabernacles and at the same time they were yearning for a homeland, a place to settle. The letter Beth encourages those who are searching for a home to sanctify or make holy the place they presently find themselves. Beth offers hope to the those seeking the freedom that the early Israelites sought and found. One way to feel at home with ourselves is to feel at home with our bodies. Beth as a home also recognizes that we must feel at home with ourselves. Beth reminds us to recognize the beauty and wonder, the holiness of our physical selves, no matter what we look like or what shape our bodies are in, it is our home while we are here on earth and we are to respect and love it.

The Beth is the first letter in the word barak ברא. This is the word for blessing. A home filled with the love of God is a blessing. Thus another meaning for the letter Beth is blessing. The Beth calls us to ponder the nature of blessing. What does a blessing mean? What does it mean to be blessed? How can we be a blessing to others. The real challenge of the Beth is to bless even if we do not feel blessed.[147]

Beth does have a shadow. There is a real danger that you become so convinced that your house is the best house that you look down on others. This is true when the house is a church. A church is a place of love and blessing it is a house that is filled with the love and blessings of God. The Shadow of the Beth warns against the notion that your house is better than other houses. The Shadow of the Beth warns against becoming spiritually proud.[148]

---

[147] Seidman, pg.24.
[148] Ibid.

We can sum of the meaning of the Beth to be:

Primary:

1. A home
2. A place filled with God's presence
3. Love
4. Our heart
5. Blessing

Shadow:

1. Spiritual pride and arrogance.

Gimmel ג

The Gimmel is the third letter of the Alphabet. The number three is often associated with God. If you take the word Gimmel גמל and add an Aleph to it you have the word Gimmela' גמלא which means a bridge uniting two areas.[149] The number three would fit the God head of the Son as Jesus who is a bridge between us and God the Father.

The word Gimmel itself means to *nourish until completely ripe.* It also means to recompense or reward. It also has the meaning of *to load* on.[150] This goes along with its noun form to mean a *camel.* The camel received its Hebrew name Gimmel because it can travel for a long time without drinking water. It can be nourished for a long time.[151] Thus you have the idea of nourishment associated with the Gimmel. The shape of the Gimmel ג is like that of a man whose feet are in motion, he

---

[149] Babylonian Talmud, Moed Katan Vol. 4 6b, pg. 33.
[150] Ibid., pg. 500.
[151] Munk, pg. 71.

is running. The feet enable a man to run and find those who are poorer than he is so he may give them nourishment. The Talmud teaches: "Because it is fitting for the benevolent to run after (seek out) the poor.[152]

The Gimmel ו has three parts to it, a head, body and foot. It is explained that the three parts represent *bestows, grow and sustains.* That is to mean that one grows to bestow kindness and nourishment to his neighbors.[153]

But this is more than just kindness by man, the Gimmel also represents the kindness of God. It represents God's eternal beneficence. Without the kindness of God the entire world would not exist for even a moment. Even death springs from God's kindness. "Whatever the All-merciful does is for the good.[154] Gimmel begins the Hebrew phrase for *lovingkindness* גמלת חסדים *gamelet hasidim.*

Gimmel begins the Hebrew words for both *exile (galut)* and paradise *(gan eden)* suggesting that our daily actions will unite two seemingly different realms. This brings us back to the idea of *gammela'* the bridge that unites or connects two areas. Thus Gimmel is teaching us that two opposing forces must be blended together to form a third more complete and perfect entity.[155]

To accomplish all this takes endurance. Again this is the picture of the camel which can endure long trips through the desert. The letter Gimmel teaches us that lovingkindness creates this endurance for us. There is the story of a hunchback street cleaner who survived the Auschwitz concentration camp. When asked how he survived he quoted his old rabbi, "Children, precious children, remember, the greatest thing in the world is to do somebody else a favor." This teaching not only helped him to endure the horrors of a concentration camp but survive again as

[152] Babylonian Talmud, Shabbat 104a, pg. 500.
[153] Kaplan, pg. 8-9.
[154] Babylonian Talmud, Berachos 60b.
[155] Scherman, pg. 74.

a street cleaner in Israel. He would comment, "Do you know how many favors you can do on the street?[156] The Gimmel teaches lovingkindness which will nourish you and give you endurance.

There is a shadow to the Gimmel, however. There is an old saying, "The road to hell is paved with good intentions." There have been many Christians in their zeal to share the love of God that have thoughtlessly brought hardship to others. In their zeal to help the poor they have sometimes brought shame and embarrassment to others. Missionaries armed with only good intentions have brought disease and cultural destruction to the people they sought to convert. The shadow of Gimmel warns us to use thoughtful and skillful means when we try to show lovingkindness.

The meanings behind the Gimmel can be summed up as the following;

Primary:

1. Lovingkindness
2. Endurance
3. Nourishment

The Shadow of the Gimmel

1. Over zealousness in trying to show kindness resulting in harm.

Daleth ד

The Daleth ד consists of two lines, one from the right to the left on the top and the other straight down on the right side.

---

[156] Seidman, pg. 28.

The inner side is hollow and empty like our physical existence. Physical existence is only a thing or an affair. The outer side of the Daleth is complete, this tells us that the Daleth appears like an open door and is an open door to spirituality. In other words the hollow empty inner side is the physical existence that provides a hiding place for the spiritual. The Daleth is then a door or portal to the spiritual world.[157]

The word Daleth דלת is related to the word *daluth* דלה which means *poverty or leanness*.[158] The physical is poor and deficient for it can receive but it cannot give. Therefore in and of itself the physical existence cannot resemble God. Only when the physical existence is coupled with the Gimmel ג, lovingkindness and mercy can the door open and the connection be made with the Divine.[159] In other words the Daleth represents a doorway that we pass through from this physical world which has its spiritual limitations, yet hidden in it is the spiritual which we enter when we pass through the Daleth. The Daleth is a doorway to the spiritual.

The Daleth represents knowledge, the doorway to the spiritual opens up knowledge of the spiritual world to us. The Bible shows that even an ordinary bush like the one on Mount Sinai can evoke an encounter with the Divine.[160] We are often so hurried in our lives and so focus on the material that we miss out on the many ordinary doorways to the spiritual world which offer us a knowledge of God. We can interpret a little bird dancing and singing our porch as a distraction which may leave a mess that we must clean up or we can pause and pass through the Daleth and realize that here is a small part of the creation of God presenting to us beauty, peace and serenity. We must

---

[157] Ben Jacob Ha-Kohen, Rabbi. Explanation of the Letters (Paulist Press), 1986, pg. 157.
[158] Babylonian Talmud, Shabbat 104a.
[159] Zohar, Vol. 1, pg. 12.
[160] Exodus 3:2 KJV.

pause in our busy lives to anticipate the many little Daleths or doorways that God will open to share with us the things of the spirit, fill what is lacking or deficient in the physical world, to take the poverty of this physical world and fill it with the blessings of God's spirit.

Related to this is the word Devekut דְּלוֹ which means *to cleave or cling to.* It is really a major form of Jewish meditation that has largely been ignored in the Christian community although it is practice among different Christian groups under a different name. The brothers at the trappest monastery I stayed in called it contemplative prayer. I once visited the church in Toronto where the Toronto Blessing occurred and I saw people practicing what they called *soaking*. Both were a form of *devekut*. Its core experience is one of intense melding or binding together with God. The Chasidic leader Rabbi Schneur Zalman describes *devekut* as habituating one's mind and thought continuously on God so that everything one sees with one's eyes, the heavens and the earth and all that is in it constitutes the outer garments of God.[161] The doorway of the Daleth is meditation upon God and upon His word.

The Talmud indicates that the Daleth ד is turned to the left, away from the Gimmel ג. This shows that the Daleth, one receiving the good works of the Gimmel, should not have to face his Gimmel or benefactor. Assistance should be given discreetly and with the greatest tact to preserve the self-respect of the recipient. In the highest form of charity, neither the Gimmel nor the Daleth should be aware of the other's identity.[162]

The Talmud teaches that in the Temple there should be a special chamber called the *Chashaim* which is the Chamber of Silence. Anyone may enter, rich or poor, but only one person at a time. Those who enter could leave a contribution to an

[161] Hoffman, pg. 31.
[162] Babylonian Talmud, Shabbat 104a.

anonymous fund or if they were needy could take from the fund discreetly.[163]

Thus the Daleth is a doorway into emptiness. In other words it is a doorway one should enter when giving or sharing mercy with others. It is to be done with the intent of receiving no reward, nothing in return. The doorway to charity is empty, giving without expecting anything in return.

The Daleth ד is also a picture of a person doubled over while carrying a heavy load. It is like a poor person who knocks on doors begging for alms. This is the poor person that the Gimmel is rushing to in order to give charity.[164]

When we meditate on the Daleth we are to consider the true nature of wealth. Daleth calls us to open up our doors to receive the blessings of God. Sometimes it is very difficult to admit that we are needy and to allow ourselves to accept offerings. Yet, the very nature of the physical world is lacking and no matter how rich or poor or how stable or unstable a person is so long as they live in this physical world, they will have needs and must open the door of the Daleth and be willing to receive the spiritual gift of God, the gift of Jesus Christ.

The emptiness beyond the Daleth reminds us that we are limited in this physical world, thus the Daleth represents humility for as we are reminded of our limitedness it should cultivate humility in us and keep us from becoming arrogant and puffed up with our own importance.

The English word *humility* comes from the word *hummus* which means earth. The Hebrew word for *human* is *adam* אדם which also means both *man* and *earth*. As we become more humble we become more human. Humility arises from being connected with our roots, down close to the soil. The bent over Daleth ד which is bent over toward the ground calls us to remember our

---

[163] Ibid, Shekalim 5:6.
[164] Seidman, pg. 33.

connection with the ground that our bodies, our nurturance and our very lives depend upon the earth. Daleth calls us to a holistic view of the world, that we are connected to this world physically and we must respect God's creation. We must consider the environment and protect the environment. We must protect all living creatures and use only what is meant by God to use to sustain our lives and not to abuse it.

The Talmud teaches that more than a baby seeks to be nursed, does a mother seek to nurse her baby. Sometimes we give, sometimes we receive, the door of the Daleth swings both ways. We must remain open to each situation and not be burdened with an overinflated idea of ourselves or excessively self-condemnatory. We must seek the appropriate response to the open door Daleth.[165]

Our senses are doorways to our bodies, as we open our senses the blessings will naturally flow. These blessings come through the sunlight reflecting off of leaves, the colors of flowers, the smell of natural fragrances, the taste of an apple. Yet, we take these simple blessings too much for granted and shut the Daleth of our senses to them. The priest in the Old Testament would burn fragrances in preparation for worship. We have learned from modern science that these fragrances such as frankincense and myrrh have a calming effect on the human body and brain. We forget that the priest were human like everyone else. They had their bad days, they had their days when they did not feel like worshipping, they would become tense, irritable, and upset. One could not worship with such feelings. By burning the incense they opened the Daleth of their senses to receive the blessings of the fragrances created by God to calm the body and mind.

---

[165] Seidman, pg. 35.

As the effects of the fragrances soothed their troubled minds, they could then be in a proper state, both physically and spiritual to worship God.[166] [167]

The Daleth is pictured as an open door. It is sending a message to us to always remain open, to keep the doors of our hearts open to the suffering and pain in this natural world. So much of our lives and modern culture is built to distract us from this suffering and pain. We would prefer not to experience or observe it, yet if we remain open we will be able to offer heartfelt prayers for the suffering and pain of this world. One teacher once wrote that it is not the words of our prayers that go up to God, it is not the words themselves. It is rather the burning desire of your heart that rises like smoke toward heaven. If your prayer consist only of words and letters and does not contain your heart's desire then how can it rise up to God?[168] The Daleth reminds us that our prayers must come from our hearts and not our physical words or speech.

The Daleth carries with it a warning or a shadow. One must be careful in his quest for humility for it may produce a false humility. There is an old story of a very humble man who was known and respected for his humility such that the king of the land gave the man a medal for his humility. The next day the king demanded that the man return the medal. When he asked why, the king said, "Because your wore it." The Daleth warns that we can easily fall prey to the human desire for recognition and praise. We may, without realizing it, nurse a desire to be praised for how noble we are for our sacrifices and modest outward behavior. We become proud of how humble we are. The Daleth stands as a subtle reminder of this tendency.

---

[166] Stewart, David, Healing Oils of the Bible, (Care Publications), 2012, pg. 291..
[167] Young, Gary, Essential Oils Desk Reference (Life Source Publishing), 2011, pg. 2.40.
[168] Seidman, pg. 36.

On the other hand there is a danger of excessive humility. Lack of self-esteem can lead to depression and self-destructive behavior. The Daleth seeks to encourage us to consider the fact that sometimes a little less humility and a little more pride may be exactly what someone may need.[169]

We can sum up the meanings of the Daleth with the following:

Primary:

1. A doorway to spiritual knowledge
2. An open door to our grief and joy
3. An open heart to the suffering and needs of the world
4. Humility
5. A doorway to our senses to receive what God has given us in the physical world to bring us healing and peace.
6. A doorway to the realization of the emptiness of the physical world.
7. A doorway to the Spiritual or God through Jesus Christ.

Shadow:

1. Excessive humility
2. False humility

Hei ה

Hei ה is the fifth letter of the Alphabet. It is used grammatically as a prefix designating a definite article (the) and as a suffix indicating a feminine gender. The word itself can be spelled two ways as הא or ה. הא means *lo, behold* or *here it is.* The Hei expresses the idea of *being* or *existence.* Rabbi Ginsburgh explained it this way, that

---

[169] Ibid., pg. 38.

this sense of being is a power of self-expression. With the power of self-expression we plant the land. Planting the land means expressing ourselves, showing our existence. Self-expression is the giving of the gift of self. The garments of our self-expression are our words, thoughts and actions. By our actions and words we bring what is in our thoughts to the awareness and consciousness of others.[170] Thus the first thing we learn about the Hei is that it is the letter of being, existence and self-expression.

The Jewish sages believed that God created the world with the Hei ה:

> Since He created them with the ה; hence I may say that this world was created with the ה. This is the revealed meaning of the letter ה.[171]

We learn from Scripture that God created the world by speaking 'amar.[172] The word 'amar אמר in Hebrew means speech or thought.[173] God created the world through self-expression. The idea of self-expression implies existence and the presence of someone or something. Hence the Hei also carries the idea of God's presence.

The Hei ה has a small gap in the upper left hand corner. This small space is very important. This small gap is a space for the light of God to reach us, no matter how dark or bad things may seem. Rabbi Nachman explains:

> Why is its left leg suspended? It is because if the sinner returns to God, he is brought up. He is brought up

---

[170] Ginsburgh, pg. 80.
[171] Babylonian Talmud, Seder Kodashim, Vol. 1, Menahot 29b (Soncino Press), 1938. pg. 191.
[172] Genesis 1.
[173] Davidson, pg. 33.

through the upper opening, between the leg within the ה and its roof. Why not bring him up through the lower opening? the one through which he went out? It will not help because when someone comes to purify himself, he needs help in overcoming the evil inclination. He is therefore aided with an additional opening.[174]

A better way to explain it is that this gap in the upper left hand corner is a window of repentance. It is the space through which we carry out our repentance and reenter the world of the living.[175]

In other words the Hei is the letter that represents the presence of God which brings us into a right relationship with Him through repentance.

From a Christian perspective we see that the ה has three parts. There is the vertical line on the left, the horizontal line on top or the roof and the vertical line on the right. We could say that the line on the left represents God the Son who connects us with the horizontal line or the roof which is God the Father and is supported by the line on the right which represents the Holy Spirit. However, the gap between the Son and Father is the opening of repentance. As we pass through the opening of repentance we enter the light and life of God through the joining of the Son with the Father.

The letter Hei is found twice in the sacred name of God YHVH יהוה. This connotes the divine revelation. Its sound resembles a mere exhalation and teaches of God's effortless breath in the formation of man. Frequently, in the Bible when God called righteous figures like Abraham or Moses they replied, הנני hineini which means, *Here I am* or *I am present*. Rabbi Nachman

[174] Nachman, Rabbi, Likutey Morharan, vol. 10, trans. Moseh Mykoff (Breslov Research Institute), 1992, pg. 37-39.
[175] Glazerson, Matityahu, Rabbi, Letters of Fire, Trans. S. Fuchs (Kest-Lebovits, Jewish Heritage and Roots Library), 1984, pg. 33.

explained that our world consists of nothing except the day and hour that we stand in now.

Tomorrow is a completely different world. The letter Hei tells us that God is present in our lives every single moment of every day of our lives. He is here and we are here with Him.

The letter Hei is most often linked with God's name as in *yah* ■'. Hei is also the mildest sounding of the letters, it is a letter that is spoken with your breathe and not your tongue. Hei whispers to us in worship that we are close the Holy Name. As Hei denotes the feminine form of a noun it represents the mothering or nurturing aspect of God. Throughout the Old Testament God is either referred to as Elohim אלהים or YHVH יהוה'. When Scripture uses the word Elohim it is referring to the masculine aspect of God, the provider, the protector, and the disciplinarian. When Scripture uses the name YHVH it is then referring to the feminine aspect of God, His nurturing, caring and loving. The Hei is a soft, gentle letter.

The Hei is also known as the broken letter. The little space in the left hand corner denotes a brokenness. As an imagine of God's presence it signifies that His presence is a soft, gentle presence, one that is easily broken. Scripture even warns us not to grieve the Holy Spirit.[176] The Holy Spirit is pictured as a dove,[177] a gentle soft bird that is easily wounded. I once had a pet dove and when he was out of his cage he would fly to my shoulder and rest on my shoulder. However, if I became agitated or upset, he would fly away because he was very easily wounded. His cooing was a soft coo that I would imitate with my breathe. The Hei is like the dove, it reminds us of the soft gentleness of the presence of God.

Hei is used as a prefix to show the definite article, *the*. The definite article indicates something specific, not just a generality or abstraction. Hei reminds us to not become lost in our

---

[176] Ephesians 4:13 KJV.
[177] Mark 1:10, Luke 3:32 KJV.

abstractions or generalities. Hei reminds us to pay close attention to the specifics.[178]

When Moses was tending his father-in-laws sheep he saw a fire coming from a bush. This was not an unusual site in the that land. Yet, he said that he was going to go over and investigate it. The Bible tells us that when he *saw that he turned aside to see, God called to Him.*[179] Moses was paying attention to the details, he noticed it and then willingly went to investigate. It was then that God called him.

The Hei is a gentle quiet letter, like a dove, it is a breathe, like a gentle breeze. The Hei reminds us to pay close attention for God may not speak to us in an earthquake, or a mighty wind, or even in fire, He may speak to us in a *still small voice* קוֹל דְּמָמָה דַקָּה. Probably the best way to describe a *qol demamah daqah* (still small voice) is to attend a professional baseball game. Sit way at the top of the stands behind home plate. The crowds will be cheering, there will be talk and confusion all around you, there will be multiple distractions but if you focus all your attention on that umpire you will actually hear him shout "Ball!" or "Strike." That is the *qol demamah daqah,* the still small voice. It is what you hear when you shut out all the distractions of the world, all the cares of this world and you focus your full attention on the Hei, the presence of God, it is then you will hear Hei whisper to you, it will be the breathe of God, His *qol demamah daqah,* His still small voice. The Hei is the *qol demamah dagah,* the *still small voice.*

The Hei is the broken letter. This is a picture that was recognized even during the time of Jesus. Could it be that when he met with His disciples during the last supper, he spoke with them esoterically as any rabbi would speak to his disciples When He announced that he was going to die, not one voice was raised in objection. Not one disciple cried out, "Nay, master it will not be."

[178] Seidman, pg. 43.
[179] Exodus 3:4 KJV.

They all just sat and listened to their master speak to them and they very likely began to think like disciples and think esoterically. What is the master really saying here. Surely, he is not talking of a literal death, but he speaks of the bread being broken as his body which he was giving to them.[180] Then he took the wine and said that it was his blood[181] Could the disciples be thinking of the broken letter, the Hei ה? The wine would picture the Yod \ Maybe Jesus was telling His disciples something even more than his death and the redemption it would bring, maybe He was also telling them, "I am Yah ה the sacred name of God Jehovah. Perhaps that is just speculation, but it does illustrate the power of the letter Hei.

The Hei comes with a shadow. As the broken letter, the Hei warns us of getting stuck in our brokenness. Broken hearts, like broken bones can cripple you.[182] Many pastors and missionaries have left their work because of a broken heart, because of the rejection of those that they devoted their lives to in ministry. The Hei whispers a warning to us to guard against a broken heart that will cripple you. That the broken letter is joined by the right line, Son of God and the horizontal line, the Father and that this brokenness can be healed by the cross where He was broken.

The Hei also warns that this still small voice is not that easy to distinguish between the voice of God and self-deception. History is littered with the dry, sun baked bones of Christians who have really thought they heard that still small voice but were only caught up in self-deception and grand illusions about themselves. The voice they heard was the voice of their own ego crying out for attention and self-gratification. The Shadow of the Hei reminds us that we must temper our confidence in our revelations with a little humility so that we do not impose our own personal visions upon that of God's.

---

[180] Matthew 26:26 KJV.
[181] Matthew 26:27-28 KJV.
[182] Seidman, pg. 45.

The summary of the meanings behind the Hei would be the following:

Primary:

1. God and us exist in the moment
2. God's presence
3. The gentleness of God
4. The broken letter showing God's act of restoration through His Son Jesus Christ.
5. Pay close attention to the specifics
6. God's still small voice

Shadow

1. Do be crippled by your brokenness
2. Pay close attention to the still small voice, beware of self-deception.

Vav ו

The sixth letter of the Alphabet is the Vav. The letter is shaped like a tent peg or nail. A peg or nail is used to connect something. The Vav in Hebrew grammar is a conjunction which could be rendered *and, or, nor* and is a prefix to a word. It can also be a conversive prefix, that is one which can time switch or shift a verb from the pasts to the future or the future into the past. In other words this is a letter that signifies a connection. The Vav transcends time and the natural to the supernatural. It is a connection between heaven and earth.

The Vav is a reflection of the tower of Babel. The tower of Babel was intended to physically unify heaven and earth by establishing a city in which all the people would live together and not be scattered throughout the earth. The symbol of this unification would be a tower that would reach up into the heavens on which they would make a name for themselves. In this case the word *vav* name means idol. They would build a tower in which they would wage war against God as this unification would be void of God.[183] The Vav is telling us that such a unification is impossible as it can only be accomplished with God. Unification and connection cannot succeed in the natural without a connection to the supernatural. The Vav reminds us of the importance of a connection with God to be unified.

Every year hundreds and thousands of churches split or are torn apart because they fail to unify. The body tries very hard to have a sense of unity but when they look to the natural rather than look to their connection with heaven personal and petty differences become magnified. They begin speaking different languages. One may speak a language of growth, another of finances, another of ministry, another of personal glory. Yet, when they forget the Vav, their connection to heaven and seek to glorify their body, their denomination, their personal theology, their personal ambition their very attempts to build a church a tower unto heaven becomes a source of personal pride and when they speak different languages of personal agendas, they scatter. The Vav unifies and connects us to heaven.

The numerical value of the Vav is six. This is very significant for the world has six directions, north, south, east, west, above and below. The Vav is nothing other than six directions.[184] These six directions are the physical side to the spiritual. The world was created and sealed with six directions in six days. The first word in the Book of Genesis has six letters *bereshith* בְּרֵאשִׁ֖ית.

---

[183] Midrash Rabbah, Genesis, Vol. 1 pg. 305.
[184] Kaplan, pg. 30.

The Vav begins the sixth word of the Book of Genesis. This is considered to show that God was making his connection from heaven to earth.[185]

In the book or Revelations we learn that the number of man is six.[186] Six is the number that made the connection of heaven to earth, yet earth may have the six directions, but heaven has seventh direction, eternity. Time for earth will end, but time for heaven has no end.

The Vav is the Hebrew prefix for *and.* This conjunction joins together words, sentences and concepts. Vav tells us that things which seem to be separate and even contradictory, such as you find in a conflict, can be viewed as comprising a higher unity. With the right attitudes you can perceive the nature of the unity and resolve the conflict.[187]

Another aspect of the Vav is that it has a straight upward form. This suggest a uniqueness. We are to seek a uniqueness with God. The Baal Shem Tov once said:

Never seek to imitate the spiritual path of another. If you try to do so, not only will you fail in fulfilling your own path, but you will not do as well in the task meant for your neighbor.[188]

I have seen in many churches, particularly those who call themselves Full Gospel or Charismatic, where there is some manifestation of the Spirit of God. Perhaps it is in a groaning, a falling under the power of the Spirit of God, laughing, grunting, or even crying. I have no question that the Spirit of God may choose to manifest Himself in such ways, but what often happens

---

[185] Ginsburgh, pg. 94.
[186] Revelation 13:18.
[187] Hoffman, pg. 36.
[188] Ibid.

is someone sees someone rolling in the aisle or running laps around the church and they think, "Well, I can do that." So they start to roll in aisle, fall under the power or run laps around the church. But all they are doing is imitating someone else; they are not looking to see what special way the Holy Spirit may choose to manifest Himself in them. Not only will they miss their own spiritual path but they will cheapen and disrupt the path of the one who is really moving under the Spirit of God. The Vav is telling us to find our connection to heaven in that special way that God created us to find our connection. God is an infinite God and He has infinite ways for us to connect with heaven. No two Vavs can be exactly alike, even if you trace it there will still be some difference, if not on a microscopic level. God does not have a set list of ways to manifest Himself in our lives, He may duplicate some experiences but still He created each of us unique and different so He can reveal himself in one of His many infinite ways of revelation. Our problem is that we live in the six directions of the natural world which has limits and therefore we can only think in terms of a God who has limits in his ability to reveal Himself and manifest Himself. Yet, when the Vav connects us to heaven, in that connection we can experience the seventh direction which taps us into the infinite and thus we can experience God and a manifestation of God like no other on earth that is living, has lived or will live. The Vav reminds us that we are unique in God, one has ever existed like us.

The Vav as the number six, the number of man, reminds us that God has built in the power of connection. Many diseases or mental illnesses are the result of a feeling of disconnection. Our modern Western society is a society that breeds on disconnection. In the ancient world people depended upon the neighbors to protect them from bandits, to put out fires, to help gather food when they are ill or disabled. In the New Testament we find that when Jesus asked a man to follow him he said that he must first bury his father.[189] This is a little difficult for us to understand in our modern Western disconnected culture. The first century people of the Near East did not have a fire department to put out their fires, they did not have a police department to protect them or a welfare system to take care of them if they become disabled, they had to depend upon each other. They were much more holistic in their thinking. This man's father was not dead, but was probably too elderly to take care of himself and this son felt his first duty was to be with his father before following Jesus. When Jesus said, Let the dead bury the dead, he was using an old Aramaic idiom which was a reference to the community, if this man did follow Jesus, which would be only for a few months according to custom, the community he lived in would take care of his father. Many in the community were blood related to begin with.

The point is that many in the ancient world and even in third world nations today have a more holistic approach to life than we in this culture do. Yet, the Vav is calling out to us to stay connected, stay connect with your family, your neighbors, friends, and community. Stay connect with all that God has given you on this earth to meet your needs for a healthy and satisfied life.

The Vav not only calls us to connect with heaven, but with those around us as well. The words of John Donne expresses this very well:

> All mankind is one author, and is one volume; when one man dies, one chapter is not torn out of the book, but translated into a better language... As therefore the bell that rings to a sermon, calls not upon the preacher only but upon the congregation to come: so this bell calls us

---

[189] Luke 9:59, Matthew 8:21 KJV

all: but how much more me, who am brought so near the door by this sickness. *no man is an island,* entire of itself.. .any man's death diminishes me, because I am involved in mankind; and therefore never send to know *for whom the bell tolls; it tolls for thee.*"[190]

The bells of the message of God tolls for all, the Vav reminds us that even though it connects to heaven, we are still connect to this earth and those who inhabit this earth. The Vav reminds us that we have a responsibility to share the message of the salvation of Jesus Christ who all who inhabit this planet with us.

The Vav has its shadow and warnings. The shape of the Vav is like that of a hook. The Vav is warning against getting hooked on something. Addictions of all sorts are a kind of overconnected-ness. Thus, the Vav is warning against becoming too connected with things like drugs, alcohol or even smoking. Yet, the Vav is even more subtle, there are addictions that we are not even aware of, personal praise, work, stimulation, or our own personal melodramas.

The Vav warns against a co-dependence. We can become overly connected with a person such that we no longer nourish our own unique individuality. Thus the Vav is warning us against addictions and an unhealthy co-dependence upon someone.

The meaning of the Vav in summary is:

Primary:

1. A connection with heaven and earth
2. A connection with those who share the world with us.
3. A uniqueness in our experience with God

---

[190] Donne, John, Meditations XVII, 1624. Devotions Upon the Emergent Occasions and Seuerall Steps in my Sickness.

Shadow:

1. Addiction
2. Unhealthy co-dependence

Zayin ז

The Zayin is the seventh letter of the Hebrew Alphabet and has the numerical value of seven. The word Zayin is spelled זין and means arms or weapons. The Zayin ז is even shaped like a sword, with the top being the hilt and the vertical part being the blade. Weapons are used to bring peace from those who are opposing peace. Arms are used to settle a conflict over possessions, something like land, resources or food. The word in Hebrew for *war* is *Milhamah* מלחמה. What is central to war? It is found in the center of the Hebrew word for war לחם *Lechem* this is the Hebrew word for bread. Wars are fought over the very basic need to survive, often it involves food.[191] This aspect of the Zayin is associated with movement since we arm ourselves to either make movement or prevent movement.[192]

The word Zayin זין is often associated with a vulgar slang meaning which is to lie with a woman. It is often used for a *fornicator, lecher and womanizer*. It is related to the word zayiyan זייין which refers to sexual intercourse. To lie with a woman in this sense is to make a movement and a connection without love, which also defines a selfish act verses movement and connection with love.[193] Thus, one of the meanings behind the Zayin is movement and peace.

The Zayin is the number seven. Many of the symbols of the Sabbath are connected with the number seven. The candles, wine,

---

[191] Blech, pg. 107.
[192] Haralick, pg. 103.
[193] Ibid.

bread, meat and fish all in some way with their Hebrew word connects to the number seven within the Gematria.[194] So ironically
where the Zayin suggest movement it also suggest rest.

The Zayin begins the word for *time zmar* זמר. Time involves
movement. Time is the key feature of human reality. Time does
not exist in the supernatural realm of God, in fact God invented
time and established time, but He lives outside of time. Yet, from
the beginning of creation He established time with seven days of
the week including the Sabbath. The Zayin teaches us that time
cannot be destroyed or even nullified as a key force in our human
existence, but it can be sanctified. Thus, Zayin also begins the
word for remember, *zachar* זכר.[195] The Zayin reminds us that our
natural existence is subject to time and that time will one day
cease. We must use our time wisely. This natural state is our only
chance to experience redemption for in eternity we will not need
redemption. It is our only chance to praise God in the midst of
trouble for in eternity trouble will be no more. It is the only time
to experience the soothing presence of God in time of sorrow, for
in eternity He shall wipe away all tears.[196]

The Talmud teaches that if someone studies Torah, helps the
poor, and dedicates his deeds to God as indicated by the first six
letters of the Alphabet, the letter Zayin offers the first level of his
reward, *God will sustain him*[197] The Zayin reminds us that God
has provided all we need when he created this world, He will sustain us or protect us. Thus the Zayin also means to *protect and
sustain*. As a sword the letter Zayin is a symbol of power. It is the
power of God that will protect us and sustain us.

As indicated with the Vav, it represents the six physical
directions of north, south, east, west, upward and downward.

---

[194] Glazerson, pg. 140.
[195] Hoffman, pg. 39-41.
[196] Revelation 21:4.
[197] Babylonian Talmud Shabbat 107b.

The Zayin represents the number seven which is the number of *completeness*. The Zayin represents the seventh direction, *inward*. This is not a physical inward but a spiritual inwardness, an inwardness of the heart and spirit which is joined with God through the atoning work of Jesus Christ. Without the atoning work of Jesus Christ our spirits are filled with sin which is not compatible with God, so it took the work of Jesus on the cross, the greatest example of the Zayin of all, for he gave his life to protect us, provide for us, sustain us and bring us rest. This was a violent act as is pictured with the sword or the Zayin, but it is used as the Zayin intended that is to bring peace.

The Zayin creates a paradox, a weapon of war is also the symbol of peace. The challenge of the Zayin is to somehow integrate the two. Can we be "peaceful warriors?" Can we wield the sword appropriately, defending and inspiring life and beauty instead of causing more death, destruction and alienation?[198] I believe Jesus gave us that example when he came to earth and brought peace to mankind through a violent act upon Himself.

So the Zayin shows us movement, peace, protection, sustenance, remembrance that our time here is short and a means of atonement to find peace with God, but it also gives us a warning, a shadow. Zayin teaches us that God will bring us rest and peace, however, too much rest and pleasure will put us out of balance. The Zayin represents seven, the seventh day, the Sabbath, the day of rest, but it reminds us there are six other days that we must work and continue our movement.

Zayin symbolizes the sword. There is a danger of too much aggression. It is important to wield the sword that defends boundaries and protects what needs to be protected without becoming violent and paranoid.[199]

The meanings of the Zayin are summed up with the following:

[198] Seidman, pg. 56.
[199] Ibid., pg. 58-59.

Primary:

1. Movement
2. Peace
3. Protection
4. Sustenance
5. Remembrance that our time is short.
6. A means of atonement and reconciliation with God has been provided.

Shadow:

1. Overindulgence
2. War and inappropriate aggression.

Cheth ‎ח

Cheth is the eight letter of the Alphabet. Where seven is the number of completion eight signifies a time of new beginnings, the entering of a new cycle. With the eighth day a new week begins. With the eighth note on a musical scale you begin a new octave, a new sound. The Hebrew word for *new* is chadash ‎חדש. The letter Cheth represents new beginnings.

The six represents man, seven represents the divine and now eight, the Chet represents a binding together of the natural man with the divine.[200] Chet represents a binding together of man with God. In fact if you look at the Chet ‎ח, it has two vertical lines or Vavs connected to a horizontal line or roof. This indicates a connection with the earth and heaven. This connection follows from the earth through the vertical line, through the heavens, the horizontal line back down to the earth through the second horizontal

---

[200] Monk, pg. 12.

line. Creating a new beginning on earth with a relationship with God. Jesus Christ has provided this connection between heaven and earth to give us a new beginning, a new life with an attachment to both heaven and earth.

Cheth is spelled Chet, Yod, Taw ח'ת, if you take the full numerical value of the word for Taw as it is spelled out Chet ח'ת, Yod יוד, and Taw תו you have full numerical value of 844. In Deuteronomy we learn why Moses was not allowed to enter the promise land, it was because he did not *sanctify* God in the presence of the children of Israel.[201] The word used in Hebrew is קדש which is the second person masculine plural Piel imperfect form for the root word *kodesh* קדשתם. *Kodesh* means *to make holy, sanctify, consecrate or to revere as holy.*[202]

When the Cheth tells us that we can bind ourselves to God through Jesus Christ and start a new beginning here on earth, the Cheth is also reminding us that whatever we do we must remember to make it holy, to revere God as holy. This means that whatever we do or think it is to be dedicated to the service of God, whatever we do as unto God. King David confirms this in his Psalm where he says; "I have set the Lord always before me."[203] The Chet reminds us that whatever we do we do as unto God.

That is why you will see orthodox Jews always wearing a kippah or skull cap. They wear it to remind themselves that they are always in the presence of God and that whatever they do they do as unto God. Many Christian clergy will wear some sort of garment that is considered sacred. Ultimately they wear it, especially during a religious ceremony to remind themselves that what they are doing they do as unto God. Even in the secular world this is a common practice. A judge will put on a robe before making a verdict and declaring a sentence reminding himself that what he is doing

---

[201] Deuteronomy 32:50-51, KJV.
[202] Zalman, Tanya, pg. 23.
[203] Psalms 16:8, KJV.

is done under the laws of the land. In some countries a judge will place a cap on his head to remind himself that he is subject to the laws of the land and what he is about to announce is the verdict of the laws of the land and not of his own personal persuasion.

Even the letter Cheth ח itself has a roof, covering or kippah over it to remind us that whatever we do we are doing as unto God and that we are always in the presence of God.

The word Chet חֵי is closely related to the word *Chaim* חַיִּים. The word Chaim means *life*. The prophet Isaiah declares that God is to be exalted because He is the *living* God who dwells on high.[204] The Cheth reminds us that God is a living God and the Cheth stands for *life*.[205] It is not seen in the standard Hebrew text used by our Christian Seminaries and Bible Colleges, but in the Jewish version of Genesis 47:28 which records Jacobs death the Cheth is enlarged in וַיְחִי יַעֲקֹב which is rendered as, *and Jacob lived*. This is done to make an allusion to the Talmudical saying that Jacob did not die but continued to live on through his descendants and on to eternity.[206] Thus the Chet not only tells us that God is living, but that man will live for eternity as well. In the English the letter 8 when placed sideways it is the symbol of infinity. A reminder that the Chet is the number 8 and represents infinity.

Chet is also the symbol of transformation. The Chet is the first letter in *chupah* חֻפָּה which is the wedding canopy. In fact the Chet ח resembles a canopy or chupah. The chupah is both a shelter and a gateway to the journey of married life. When the couple stands beneath the chupah are in a holy place an in between place. When they emerge from the chupah they are married, their lives are transformed, they belong to one another, they are no longer single but a unit.[207] The Chet is a letter that teaches transformation.

---

[204] Isaiah 33:5, KJV.
[205] Babylonian Talmud, Menachos 29b.
[206] Ibid., Ta'anis 5b.
[207] Seidman, pg. 62.

The Chet sums up our experience with Jesus. We move from this natural realm into the supernatural realm through Jesus Christ to a binding together with God. We accept Jesus Christ as our savior we are born again, transformed and experience a new beginning in Jesus Christ. Just as God has eternal life, we too will now have eternal life with Him through Jesus Christ.

Even though the Chet reminds us of life and new beginning, it also comes with a shadow. This newness in life, this special relationship with God through our bonding with him can turn to arrogance and rudeness. Although a new life in Jesus Christ is wonderful, we can become addicted to newness. We are always craving a new experience, a new thrill or a new rush in our relationship with God. Christians will spend thousands of dollars to travel across the country to some convention or seminar where they have heard there is a special anointing of God or a special presence of God. These Christians have become addicted to newness and are constantly craving something new without learning to be satisfied with their relationship with God as they experience it at the moment.

The meaning of the Cheth can be summed up as follows:

Primary:

1. New Beginnings
2. Binding with God
3. Whatever we do we do as unto God.
4. We are always in the presence of God
5. God is living
6. We have eternal life in God through Jesus Christ.

Shadow:

1. Arrogance and rudeness
2. Becoming addicted to newness.

Teth ט

Teth is the ninth letter of the Hebrew Alphabet and has the numerical value of nine. The Teth ט

Has the shape of a container that has a small opening at the top. This small opening is a funnel through which the power of God can flow into us and thereby He can share His goodness with us.[208] The Teth begins the word *Tov* טוב which means good or to be in harmony with someone. We learn that when God created the world he saw that it was *tov, good or in harmony with Him*. When we allow God to flow through the funnel of the Teth he brings us into harmony with Him.

The Teth reminds us that it is good, that whatever He does He does it to bring us into harmony with Him.[209] The Talmud teaches of Nahum of Gamzu. He was blind in both eyes, paralyzed, his body was covered in boils and they had to suspend his bed in the air with bed post sitting in pans of water to keep the insects from crawling up the post onto his bed and onto his body. In this state he still declared, "This is also for the best."[210] Nahum of Gamzu understood that all that afflicted him was meant to bring him into harmony with God and for Nahum of Gamzu, to be in harmony with God was worth all his affliction.

Rabbi Nachamn teaches:

> When things go well, it is certain good. But when you have troubles, it is also good. For you know that God will eventually have mercy, and the end will be good [bring you into harmony with God]. Everything must be good for it all comes from God.[211]

---

[208] Haralick, pg. 129
[209] Babylonian Talmud, Berakoth 60b.
[210] Ibid., Ta'anit 21a.
[211] Kaplan, pg. 125.

The Cheth reminds us that no matter what happens in our lives God will use it for *tov, good or to bring us into harmony* with Him.[212]

The Teth ט is like a vessel with an inward oriented shape. This is suggesting the goodness is often hidden in our universe. The Zohar remarks, "good is concealed within it."[213] When troubles come or we go through a difficult time, it is often very hard to see how such a situation can bring us into harmony with God. This is not to say that God causes the bad things in life to happen to us. The Teth reminds us that God is the source of all that is good. He is the source in which everything seeks to be in harmony with Him. So God may not bring the troubles upon us, but He is an opportunist who can assure us that no matter what the situation is, it can be used to bring us into harmony with Him.

The word Teth ט׳ת is closely associated with the word for travel ט׳ל. The sages would teach that travel has a spiritual potential. Each person is destined from heaven to be in a particular place at a particular time. The sages teach that if you would not make the journey voluntarily, you would have to go in chains. The philosopher Martin Buber once said, "Every journey has a secret destination of what the traveler is unaware."[214] Travel exposes us to experiences and influences outside our personal realm. It allows us to broaden our understanding and see new glories in the creation of God. The more we see of the wonders of God's creation when we travel, the more this will bring us into harmony (good) with Him. Thus, the Teth encourages us to travel and experience the broad wonders of God.

Another way of viewing the Teth ט is that it is shaped like the womb of a woman. The Teth is the number nine, which reflects the nine months of pregnancy. This letter of goodness,

---

[212] Romans 8:28, KJV.
[213] Hoffman, pg. 44.
[214] Ibid., pg. 46.

harmony with God carries the thought of gestation and the potential of life.[215] Indeed, when we go through those dark periods in our lives, it is like a gestation period, a period that is being used to prepare us for life. In every situation, no matter how bad, there is the promise of life, either in this world or the world to come. No matter what the situation there is the potential for life itself.

The Teth ט appears like a snake coiled in on itself. We have a story in the Old Testament where Moses, fashions an image of a snake and sets it on a pole. Anyone bitten by a poisonous snake need only look upon the bronze serpent and they would be healed.[216] The symbol of two snakes or double headed snakes entwined around a staff is an ancient one, predating Israel. It symbolized the potential mingling of the masculine and feminine. This image even survives today as the caduceus, the seal of Aesclepius, the wand of Hermes and as the sign of the medical profession. The Teth is a kind of caduceus which is bringing things into harmony with each other. The people in the wilderness would look upon the snake in the wilderness to be healed. This act of faith brought them into harmony with God who was then able to heal them. The two snakes intermingling on the post symbolized the mingling of a man and woman coming into harmony with each other. And the caduceus used as a symbol of medical research signifying the use of the medical profession to bring a body back into harmony with the world around them. Again we are brought back to the basic meaning of the Teth and that is goodness or bringing ourselves into harmony with God.

Yet, despite the Teth's noble declaration of goodness, it comes with a shadow. We can apply positive thinking on a superficial level. We can blithely say, "Oh it is all for the good" and ignore the pain and suffering. This may cause the Teth's shadow to arise

---

[215] Seidman, pg. 69.
[216] Numbers 21:6-9.

with more force, it may increase in the pain and suffering by ignoring the obvious things that can be done to improve the situation. When a hurricane hits and causes massive destruction, it is foolish to say, "Well, it is for the best." The good many be hidden in our efforts to relieve the suffering, to band together with neighbors and friends, to sacrifice our own resources. The Teth is teaching us not to see only good in every situation but to discover the possibilities that may arise to enhance the good or to perform actions which would bring us into harmony with God.

The Teth also warns us of imposing our positive thinking on others. We run the risk of blaming them for their circumstances, saying their illness or accident is all their own fault. Or accusing them of not having a positive attitude. The Teth is teaching us a balance, not a polarization. Teth teaches acceptance, not denial; groundedness, not fanaticism and awareness, not sentimentality.

The meanings behind the Teth are summed up with the following:

Primary:

1. Goodness, harmony with God
2. All that God does is good, it is used to bring us into harmony with Him.
3. We must allow God to funnel His goodness into us.
4. Travel to see the wonders of His creation.

Shadow:

1. Overemphasizing goodness
2. A False positive thinking

Yod ׳

The Yod is the tenth letter of the Hebrew Alphabet and has a numerical value of ten. Yod is spelled Yod, Vav, Daleth, יוד. It is closely associate with the word Yad יד which means hand, power and strength. It is also related to the word Yada ידע which means to know in the sense of being intimate with someone or something. It is the word also used for sexual intercourse. The hand is the hand of a craftsman who creates with his power or strength, the strength of the hand and the creativity of the mind comes from the spiritual realm. The intimacy in knowing comes from the sharing of your heart which is not tangible but spiritual.

The Yod ׳ is suspended in the air. It is the smallest letter, it is very easy to go unnoticed. It is barely larger than a dot. It has no component parts, so it is a letter that cannot be divided. In careful examination the Yod ׳ has top point directed toward heaven, the bottom is directed to the earth and the middle unites the two points. As the smallest letter it symbolizes the spiritual realm. The spiritual realm is not easy to notice and passes out attention. The Bible teaches that we wrestle not against flesh and blood but against principalities, against powers, against the rulers of the darkness of this world, against spiritual wickedness in high places. [217]How often we lash out against the circumstances, the people or the organization that is causing us difficulty and pain distracting us from our relationship with Him, distracting us from the Teth, the goodness of God.

Yet, all along the letter Yod that follows Teth comes as a reminder that we are not fighting against natural things, but against spiritual forces bent on destroying the Teth, the harmony we have with God.

---

[217] Ephesians 6:12-13. KJV.

The Yod floating in the air is a reminder to us to keep looking up, looking to heaven. We have the story of the Israelites fighting with the Amalekites.[218] It is Moses upheld hand that initiates God's help, making the Israelites prevail. Scripture teaches that when Moses held his hand יָ or his Yod up that Israel prevailed. And when he let his hand יָ or Yod down the Amalekites prevailed.

The Talmud teaches that us that it was not the physical act of holding up his hand that initiated God's help. Holding up his hand was the means by which Moses communicated to the Israelites to keep their thoughts tuned to the above and to subject their hearts to God. It was the turning of their thoughts to the above and the subjecting of their hearts to the will of God that was the direct cause for God's help.[219] The Yod reminds us to keep looking above, keep looking at God as our source for the Teth, the goodness.

C.S. Lewis stated in Mere Christianity:

> In God you come up against something which is in every respect immeasurably superior to yourself. Unless you know God as that and, therefore, know yourself as nothing in comparison you do not know God at all. As long as you are proud you cannot know God. A proud man is always looking down on things and people: and, of course, as long as you are looking down, you cannot see something that is above you.[220]

Here C.S. Lewis has given a perfect illustration of the Yod. The Yod reminds us to always look up for when you are looking down, down on the cares and problems of this world, how can you see

---

[218] Exodus 17:11, KJV.
[219] Babylonian Talmud, Rosh Hashanah 29a.
[220] Lewis, C.S., Mere Christianity, Chapter 8, The Great Sin (Harper and Row), 2009.

what is above you. The Yod not only expresses spirituality but also reminds us to keep looking up.

The numerical value of the word Yod is twenty (Yod = 10, Vav = 6, and Daleth = 4). The word *Ha'aviv* האביב also has a numerical value of 20. *Ha'aviv* is the month on the Jewish calendar that initiates spring, the month for the celebrating of the feast of the unleavened bread. This celebrates the deliverance from the wilderness and from darkness. Like the ending of winter there is the promise of a spring when everything seems to come alive again after you have gone dormant during the winter months. Yod reminds us that there is hope when we look up.

You will find that many of the Biblical names of prophets and leaders started with the letter Yod, such as Yisroel (Israel), Yacov (Jacob), Yehoshua (Joshua), Yoel (Joel), Yoneh (Jonah), Yehezekiel (Ezekiel), Yirmiyahu (Jeremiah) and Yeshaya Isaiah.[221] All these Old Testament heroes had two things in common, they all looked up to receive their directions. They all looked to God to guide them. The second thing they had in common was that they brought about change. Just one speck in the midst of millions brought about change, just as the Yod is the smallest letter, seemingly insignificant, yet it is a mighty and powerful letter. The Yod reminds us that even the smallest and most insignificant among us can be used by God to accomplish great things. We look to the Yod to remind us that we are never too small to be used by God.

The Bible commands us to love the Lord God with all our hearts. [222]Just what does that mean with *all* our hearts? There is a word in Hebrew, yetzer יצר which means *an impulse*. The Yod teaches us that we are born with tendencies for *selflessness (yetzer hatov) and selfishness (yetzer hara)*. God commands us, in fact the greatest commandment of all is love the Lord God with all your impulses, both selfless and selfish. The tendency to love God with

---

[221] Hoffman, pg. 47.
[222] Luke 10:27, Deuteronomy 6:5.KJV.

all your *yetzer hatov* (selflessness) is easy to understand. We are to serve God with no selfish motives, no hidden personal agendas. Yet we are to also love God with our *yetzer hara (selfishness).* The Talmud teaches that it is the *yetzer hara* our personal passion and momentum that leads us to marry, to build a house, to beget children or engage in business.[223] The Yod reminds us that the *yetzer hara* does not have to be evil, it can be directed to God. That is why we must love the Lord God with all our hearts with both our selfish and unselfish desires. For even our selfish desires can be directed to God.

The Yod is the symbol of friendship. The word Yod יוד is closely related to and associated with the word Yad, יד. Yad is the word for hand. The ancients believed your heart was in the palm of your right hand. It was your hand that you performed physical labor, it was your hand that you extended to help another, your strength and power was manifested in your hand. Thus a handshake in ancient times was far more than the meeting of fingers, it was the sharing of one's heart. When the Jews wish to show their love for God they place phylacteries on their arms to subjugate all that they do to the service of God with all their heart. A true friend and a beloved friend is יד יד Yadiyad. The word Yad יד is repeated twice, hand in hand. The closeness in the hands demonstrates the nearness of hearts. One hand יד has a numerical value of 14 (Yod = 10, Daleth = 4), two hands equal 28. The numerical value of the word for strength כח (Kap = 20, Cheth = 8) also equal 28. In friendship there is strength beyond compare.[224] The Yod reminds us that there is strength in friendship with both God and man.

If you recall the Cheth ח is a picture of a chupah, the marriage canopy. This is followed by the Teth ט which is the picture of the womb, giving birth or the gestation period. The next letter to follow in the alphabet is the Yod which in its root form also means

---

[223] Hoffman, pg. 49.
[224] Blech, pg. 135.

to thrust. After marriage of the Cheth and the conception and gestation of the Teth we come to the Yod which *thrust its way into existence.*[225] As noticed earlier the Yod is suspended in the air. The Talmud teaches that God used the letter Hei to create the world and He used the letter Yod to create the world to come.[226] In fact, grammatically the Yod is used to prefix a word to denote a future tense. Thus, the Yod is there to remind us that we have a future home, a home in the heavens with God. We need to remember that the Yod is also the smallest letter, easily overlooked. We must never overlook that our future home is in heaven, we are but ambassadors in this world, here on a mission from the Father in heaven who will one day be called to be with Him in that eternal state.

Despite the wonderful message of the Yod, there is a warning a shadow. The Yod floating in the air reminds us to beware of becoming ungrounded, not having a foundation. In the mid-twentieth Century there was a flood of celebrities becoming Christians and Christian organizations were fighting over each other to secure a speaking engagement from these now converted celebrities. Right after they accepted Jesus as their Savior they were sudden thrown into the spotlight on Television and radio. Christian book publishers eagerly signed them up to write their autobiographies and share their testimonies. Christians tuned into their favorite Christian television stations anxious to discover who the next new celebrity would appear that had now become a born again Christian. Yet, all too often these celebrities proved to be no different than the man on the street. They were just as human as the rest of us. Soon we would hear reports of alcoholism, drugs, divorce, scandals and even out right denial of their once new faith. What happened is that in our rush to claim these celebrities as our own we forgot to give them a foundation,

---

[225] Seidman, pg. 77.
[226] Ibid., pg. 78.

we forgot to give them a chance to grow in their Christian walk. These celebrities, just new babes in Christ were being called up to offer spiritual guidance and direction before they themselves had a chance to develop a Spiritual foundation of their own.

The Yod warns us to not be hasty in our spiritual walk, to make sure we are grounded in our faith to become a part of a church body where other believers can encourage us, guide us, pray for us and even teach us from their own experience and walk with God.

Another warning of the Yod is that we may be looking up too much and not seeing the needs that lie below. I do not like the saying, "He is so heavenly minded that he is of no earthly good." Yet, the Yod does warn of this happening. The Yod is teaching us to have a balance, to always be looking up but to always be aware of what is below and be ready to reach out with your Gimmel, lovingkindness to provide for those in need.

I would summarize the meanings behind the Yod as:

1. Spirituality
2. We are in a spiritual battle
3. We look up for or hope
4. We are never too small to be used by God.
5. There is strength in friendship with God and man.
6. Our future home is in heaven.

Shadow:

1. Build a foundation in your Christian faith.
2. Do not look up so much that you do not see the needs below.

Kap כ

Kap is the eleventh letter of the Hebrew Alphabet and has a numerical value of twenty. There is a final form which can take a value of either 20 or 500. When you look at the value of the word for the letter Yod יוד (Yod = 10, Vav = 6, Daleth = 4) you a have a numerical value of 20. This suggest a relationship between the Kap and the Yod. One relationship is that the Kap holds the Yod in the air, the other is that Kap receives a message the message from heaven that the Yod brings. The Kap is shaped like a container that is empty and ready to be filled. With a numerical value of 20, it is ready to be filled with the Spirit of God from heaven.[227]

We learn that when Jesus was baptized the Spirit of God descended upon Him like a dove.[228] The word in Hebrew for dove is Yona יונה which starts with a Yod. The Yod descended upon Jesus as the Kap and filled Him.

Grammatically the Kap is a prefix meaning *as, like, when at about or according to.* The letter offers a sense of comparison. The word itself for Kap is כף. This is the word for palm, hollow of the hand, a pan, dish or a container full of valuable contents. It also means a clip, rock or cape. It has the idea of a high point. One lifts his palm to heaven to receive. The Kap lifts up to receive what the Yod is bringing from heaven. Thus, the Kap reminds us that when we reach up to God we should anticipate receiving His presence and being filled with His presence.

When we are filled with the presence of God he inhabits our consciousness and our consciousness becomes a sanctuary for God. It is there that God reigns.[229] When God reigns in us, when the King who is above reigns in us, then we who are below

---

[227] Haralick, pg. 163.
[228] Matthew 3:16, KJV.
[229] I Corinthians 6:19, KJV.

become a king. This is our crowning achievement.[230] The Kap reminds us that our crowning achievement is that we are a temple that God inhabits.

The shape of the Kap כ is curved and bent. The word Kap כף comes from the root word כפף which means to bend, bow, show submission. The letter itself is a picture of bending over. The word also means to be hungry. The Kap כ is like a vessel or mouth looking to be filled, it is empty and hungry. It longs to be satisfied with a hunger for God.

The Kap is the first letter in כבוד kabod which means the glory of God. It is the glory of God that fills this empty vessel. It is the hunger for the glory of God that the mouth of the Kap is open to receive.

God comes to Moses after he was on the mountain top. We learn that while on the mountain top Moses spoke with God face to face as a friend would speak with the friend and after this Moses gives a strange request, he asks to see the ways of God so that he can know Him.[231] I mean who could not know God more than Moses, after all his experiences with God he still does not know Him. Moses qualifies his request and says, "Show me your *kabod* כבד." Isn't that what Moses was experience all that time on the mountain top? Moses was a Kap, a vessel longing to be filled with all that the Yod had. The word *kabod* has a wide range of meanings, it means, *respect, honor, glory splendor, majesty, reverence, distinction, importance, wealth, riches and ambition.* Yet even when we run out of English words, we still have not defined *kabod.* We can only discern from Scripture that *kabod* is a reference to the revealed presence of God. Is there any word in the English language that can describe that? It is a presence that fills all the earth and yet it is a presence that can be in the midst of a cloud that covers it. It is a presence that

---

230 Haralick, pg. 167.
231 Exodus 33:13, KJV

can be on the top of a mountain, appearing like a devouring fire. Maimonides teaches us that the glory is:

> Sometimes intended to signify the created light that God causes to descend on a particular place in order to confer honor upon it in a miraculous way.[232]

The Kap represents our crowning achievement. This is to be filled with the glory of God. It is something that we cannot define or even describe, it is something that must be experienced as with Moses. It is something that not even Moses had yet experience after the burning bush, the confrontation with Pharaoh, the multiple miracles of the crossing of the Red Sea, water from a rock, deliverance from their enemies, and even sitting on a mountain top talking with God face to face and yet, the Kap of Moses hungered to filled with the glory of God.

Maimonides also saw the Kap, the empty vessel as a call to another word which starts with a Kap, *kavana* כונה. *Kavana* is an emptying of one's mind of all thoughts and to see oneself as if he is standing before God.[233] *Kavana* comes from the root word *kaven* which means to aim. In other word is to prepare yourself for worship by clearing your mind of all fleshly and worldly distractions, to focus your attention upon God and God alone and then to enter into worship and prayer. I have observed many worship services where people go through the motions of worship, they have their hands lifted up, they are singing the song, and then they look at their watch, they speak to the person next to them, they try to quiet the child sitting next them or they look around to see how others are worshipping. They are not seeking the Kap, they are not reaching out to *kavana* to just lay aside all distractions and focusing their attention on God.

---

[232] Maimonides, Moses, The Guide of the Perplexed, Vol. 1, trans. Shlomo Pines (University of Chicago Press), 1963., pg. 156.
[233] Hoffman, pg. 50.

During my time of silence at the monastery I discovered a form of *kavana*. I would go to the meditation room alone. I would turn two chairs facing each other and then I would do what Maimonides suggested. I would picture Jesus sitting in the chair across from me and we would have a conversation. I would be so focused with my imagination picturing Him sitting across from me that I would not be thinking of anything else other than what I wanted to say to Jesus and what He was trying to say to me. This is a form of *kavana*, this is what the Kap is calling us to do.

The word Kap כפ means the palm of the hand. The palm of the hand is a picture of the work of our hands. This creation can literally be the work of our hands such as sewing, wood working, pottery, cooking, art or even writing as I am doing now. Kap is sending us the message that each one of us has a gift to give, each one of us has something to offer to create for the world. Whether it is meal or a work of art, God has given all us something to contribute to the world around us.

The Kap does warn us of a danger. Moses was a man of great humility.[234] This is very significant for such a man who has walked so close to God, felt his power, presence and spoke with God face to face as a man speaks with a friend, pride could easily enter. He could easily become a tyrant, he has heard the voice of God and those that do not hear God's voice must follow what Moses says. That is the root of pride. Kap warns us that we are drawing everything from the Yod, from the God of heaven, we must constantly remember this and not allow ourselves to become filled with such pride that we expect others to follow our personal wishes. The will is still with us. Moses overcame this and remained a humble man. When we are filled with the presence of God we must remember it is only the mercy of God that allows this to happen.

---

[234] Numbers 12:3, KJV.

I remember I once pastored a Baptist church during the days of the Charismatic movement. Over a quarter of the church received the Baptism of the Holy Spirit, their Kaps were filled and they could not wait to get into the church to share it. But what happened instead was people detected pride and arrogance. They felt these *Charismatics* felt they were better than the rest and were forcing them to worship God in a way that the others were not comfortable. The Kap warns us to be humble and not arrogant and willful.

The meanings behind the Kap can be listed as follows:

Primary:

1. A empty vessel waiting to be filled with the presence and glory of God
2. A longing to be filled with the presence of God.
3. A call to empty our minds of all distractions and focus on God.
4. We each have a gift to be shared with the world.

Shadow:

1. Arrogance
2. Willfulness

Lamed ל

Lamed is the twelfth letter of the Hebrew Alphabet and has a numerical value of thirty. As a prefix the Lamed can mean to, unto, into, toward, during, for, about, according to, at, by of, with, in within, each, every, as, or belonging to. All these words establish that the Lamed is providing in the physical realm a directed association or connection of one thing to or with another. The root word for the word for Lamed is למד Which means to learn, study or become familiar with. It also means to teach.

Thus the basic meaning of the Lamed is to reach out to share information, to teach. Lamed also means learning which involves a purpose. Note the shape of the letter Lamed ל it is like a hand reaching up to heaven. The Lamed is telling us that we are to reach up to heaven to receive our values and bring them down to earth to put them into action.235 The Lamed is the tallest letter, that suggest that learning and teaching the things of heaven and of God are the highest capabilities we have.236 But if you examine the Lamed closely you will find it has a bump in the middle of the letter. This is the suggestion of the heart. Indeed the word for heart is Lev, לב which is a lamed connected to a Beth which represents the heart. Learning is more than just intellectual learning, the learning of the Lamed is the kind of learning that connects to the heart to do and desire more of the knowledge of God. That is why the shape of the Lamed ל is composed of a Vav ו as a sort of tower on the top and the Kap כ for the body. The Vav is the connection to God and the connection receives a message from God to bring into the body which is the Kap and reflects our crowning achievement.237

The Lamed reminds us that no matter what our vocation in life may be, what education or learning we must experience to perform our life's task, we must always remember that whatever job we do we can perform our best by being righteous. Ultimately all knowledge we received should be in a Godly context.

The Midrash Rabbah teaches:

> Surely oppression turneth a wise man into a fool; and a gift destroyeth the understanding.

---

[235] Glazerson, pg. 50.
[236] Munk, pg. 139.
[237] Haralick pg. 180.

> When a wise man busies himself with many matters
> then his wisdom becomes confused.[238]

What this is saying is that by becoming busy with many affairs like business deals and other worldly affairs, a wise man turns into a fool. The reason for this is that our minds become so filled with the business that we forget our connection to God. That everything has a purpose and behind every purpose is our connection with God.

The Lamed expresses the idea of always moving toward learning. The Lamed as a proposition means to or toward. When Moses left Jethro's estate Jethro wished him to לך לשלום *go toward peace.* The Talmud teaches that when one takes his leave you are not to wish him to *go in peace,* but to *go toward peace.*[239] Moses grew increasingly more successful. A successful person makes progress in the direction of his goal. Hence our learning from heaven is not a onetime thing. We do not stop learning once we have graduated from Bible College or Seminary. When I was teaching in a Bible College my students would often question certain assignments suggesting that they were not relevant to their future ministry. They wanted me to teach little gems from Scripture that they could write down and use in their preaching when they became pastors. I explained that they would forget most of what I taught and they may lose their notes. If they lost their notes would that mean they wasted four years of Bible college? The idea was that they were learning how to study, how to search out the Scriptures for themselves. Learning was a lifelong process, learning was the Lamed, receiving from heaven. They would have to live every sermon they preached if they truly wanted to be an effective minister.

---

[238] Midrash Rabbah Vol 3, Exodus 6:2, trans. Lehrman (Soncino Press), 1983, pg. 105-106.
[239] Babylonian Talmud, Berachos 64a.

The word Lamed also means a *goad or a prod* that is used for guiding cattle. We cannot assume that our students always want to learn. Most of the time they need some form of motivation. That is why there is a heart on the Lamed as learning motivation is a matter of the heart. If you offer a grade as a reward you will have students do what is necessary to earn that grade. But if you appeal to the heart and show that what they learn will make then a better person before God and man, they seek knowledge for the sake of knowledge and not to earn a reward.

There is an old Rabbinical story of a student who complained to his rabbi that another student only studied Torah so he could be a great teacher and impress people with his great knowledge. The rabbi replied, "It is ok, the Torah will purify his motives." The greatest teacher is the one who loves the subject he teaches. That is why there is a heart in the letter Lamed, God will put that teaching into your heart. If you teach from the heart, others will fall in love with what you are teaching.

A great rabbi was once asked by a student to be shown the one universal way to serve God. The rabbi told him that there were so many ways to serve God, he could not tell give him one specific service. However, he did suggest this, "Everyone should carefully observe what way their heart draws them and then choose this way with all their strength."[240]

The Lamed not only gives a message to all who wish to teach but all who wish to serve the Lord, the Lamed teaches us that we are to search out the message that God has put into our hearts and it is that message that we must then share with all our hearts.[241] My brother spent fifteen years living in the jungles of Papua New Guinea, translating the Bible into the Amanad language. Most of us may like the idea of translating the Bible but we would cut short at the idea of living fifteen years in a jungle. It is not that my brother is anyone special, he simply followed his heart and God gave him a heart for the Amanad people.

[240] Seidman, pg. 92.
[241] Ibid.

The Lamed does have a shadow. I recall many Bible college students in my years of teaching who would walk into a Bible study with their Greek New Testaments and Hebrew Bibles and begin to show everyone their great knowledge. The Lamed teaches us that we must beware of intellectualism that causes us to not only look down upon others but to humiliate them. Grandiosity is a real danger for students of the Bible.

I have also had some very brilliant students who just could not learn some basic concepts of Biblical study because it somehow threatened their own theological position. They would develop tunnel vision and study only those things which would enhance their personal world view. They could argue their position with many quotes from many books, but they would refuse to listen to another person's argument. They became very narrow minded. The Lamed warns against using the knowledge received in your heart to becoming narrow minded.

The word Lamed means a prod. The Lamed warns against letting this prodding get out of hand. As a teacher I had to remind myself of the Lamed many times. I would find a student who was very brilliant and capable of much. I would find myself prodding him goading him into being more and more efficient. I would encourage him to take the Graduate Record Exam before he was ready, or to spend extra hours to develop the skills to enter a certain graduate school. All the time I was not fostering creativity, but causing exhaustion. The Lamed warns against workaholism.[242]

The meaning of the Lamed can be described as the following:

Primary:

1. Teaching
2. Learning

---

[242] Ibid., pg. 96.

3. Purpose
4. Receive your learning from the Holy Spirit
5. Learning is a lifelong process
6. Teach and learn from your heart.

Shadow:

1. Grandiosity
2. Workaholism
3. Narrow mindedness

Mem מ

The Mem is the thirteenth letter of the Hebrew Alphabet. The Mem has numerical value of forty. The Mem has a final form that is shaped like a book. The Mem מ represents a broken heart. The Mem has a little break in the lower left hand corner. Scripture tells us, "The sacrifices of God [are] a broken spirit: a broken and a contrite heart, O God, thou wilt not despise."[243] A broken heart is very dear and precious to god. When the shell of the heart is broken, then the pure heart forms. God fills the pure heart and with an outstretched arm God creates the openings through which we are delivered. This helps us understand the passage, "Arise, cry out in the night: in the beginning of the watches pour out thine heart like water before the face of the Lord:"[244] The picture of the Mem מ is like a vessel with a small hole in the bottom from which water will pour out. Our hearts are like that vessel which is filled with much pain and suffering. God has placed a little hole in the bottom of our heart to allow

---

[243] Psalms 51:17, KJV.
[244] Lamentations 2:19, KJV.

all that pain and suffering to drain out so he can refill the heart with His love and presence[245].

The closest word to the spelling of the Mem מם is the word mim מים which is the word for *water*. Water is sandwiched between the Mem מ and Final Mem ם. From this we learn that water is the carrier of the Yod י. The Yod is a messenger from heaven, a message of heaven. Water has always been viewed by ancient man as mysterious, the unknown. There is the revealed aspect of water that you can viewed from a ship, the surface with its waves, and color. This is the Mem, מ the revealed knowledge of God. Below the surface of the water was unknown to sailors, they could only imagine what lied beneath the water. They would draw up strange looking creatures from below the waters and only marvel at what the world is like beneath the sea. Indeed modern science has taken us beneath the sea to reveal a wondrous and beautiful world totally foreign to the world on the land. The Final Mem ם is shaped like a box with no openings, there is no way to get in or out. This is the hidden knowledge of God.[246]

Water reminds us of the flowing fluid of life. In many languages the *m* sound are related to sea and mother. The word mother and water are often very similar. The French word for *seas* is *mer* and the French word for *mother* is *mere*. In Hebrew the word for *sea* is *yahm* ים. The word for mother in Hebrew is *ahm* אם. For nine months we float in the salty water of our mother's womb. *Mama* is the first words a baby speaks, the sound of the *m*. The Hebrew word for tender mercy and lovingkindness is rachemim רחמים. This comes from the root word רחם rachem which is also the word for *womb*. The word for tender mercies רחמים ends with the word myim ים which is the word for water. Thus the Mem represents the mercy and lovingkindness of God.

---

[245] Kaplan, Aryeh Rabbi, Gems of Rabbi Nachman (Yeshivat Chasidei Breslov), 1980, pg. 134.
[246] Scherman, pg. 144.

The Mem is the number forty. Forty has always been considered the number to bring something to fruition. There were forty days and forty nights of rain in the story of Noah. The children of Israel wandered for forty years in the wilderness. Jesus fasted for forty days and forty nights. Forty is the length of time to reach a full cycle. The Mem reminds us that our lives run in cycles.[247]

Yet we find within the Mem a Shadow, a hidden warning. Many have been lost at sea, many have downed. The sea is a dangerous place. We speak of *drowning in our sorrows.* This is the warning of the Mem, sorrows can be as dangerous as the seas and we run the risk of drowning in our sorrows, losing our purpose for life itself.

Also we have seen in the last few years how floods have wreaked havoc on homes and lives. Water can not only be life giving it can also be destructive. The Bible speaks of *mayim chayim* or evil waters. This symbolizes hurtful or destructive passions. The Mem stands to warn us that we can be destroyed by our *mayim chayim,* our evil waters or destructive passions.[248]

The Mem and its final form can be described to represent the following:

Primary:

1. A broken heart draining out all its pain to be filled with love of God.
2. Revealed knowledge of God.
3. The Final Mem ם is the hidden knowledge of God.
4. Our lives run in cycles
5. The mercy of lovingkindness of God.

---

[247] Hoffman, pg. 58.
[248] Seidman, pg. 101.

Shadow:

1. Drowning in our Sorrows
2. Becoming flooded by our evil waters or destructive passions.

Nun ‎נ

The Nun is the fourteenth letter of the Hebrew alphabet. It carries a numerical value of fifty. The word is spelled Nun, Vav, Nun ‎נון. In Aramaic it means fish. In the Hebrew it has the idea of *sprouting, spreading, shinning.* We see the word Nun appearing in the Old Testament in the phrase ‎בן נון or Son of Nun. Joshua was the son of Nun. The word is usually translated as one who *endures or continues.*[249] Three times we see this used in the story of Joshua. [250] The son of Nun was Joshua who goes into the land and causes the children of Israel to inherit it. The father, Nun, is simply the *emergence,* he does not go into the promised land. It takes time for the *emergence* to produce something that is seeable. The Nun reminds us that we are often in a time of *emergence* and must wait for that which is seeable to appear.

If you combine the words ‎בן נון in Hebrew into one word you will have ‎בנון which is the word to build, a structure or a construction. It is the construction of a building. A construction site is a place where a structure is being erected and you are waiting for it to appear, the structure is in a state of *emergence.*[251]

The bent Nun ‎נ is a picture of God sitting on his throne and the Final form of the Nun ‎ן is a picture of the angles standing before Him. Here we have a picture of *naman (trustworthy)* ‎נאמן which begins with God sitting on His throne ‎נא sharing his

[249] Nachman, pg. 579.
[250] Deuteronomy 31:23, 1:38, 34:9.
[251] Haralick, pg. 208.

revealed knowledge נ‎ to his angels].[252] The word נאמן‎ *naman* means *trustworthy and faithful.* The Nun reminds us that God is faithful, He is faithful to give us whatever knowledge we may need.

The Talmud teaches that the bent Nun נ and the straight Nun ן are applied to man. The faithful one who is bent נ and the faithful one who is erect ן.[253] One who submits himself humbly before God's will, bending before him like the bent Nun, will stand straight and upright like the final Nun when he eventually faces the final Day of Judgment. The Nun is the letter for emergence and remaining faithful unto the final Day.

The Aramaic word Nun means *fish* and denotes *productiveness.* The fish has often been considered a symbol of abundance. The Nun reminds us that faith and faithfulness brings us a sense of abundance in our daily life. The Nun has been given the representation of faith.[254]

Jonah was swallowed by a great fish. In the name Jonah יונה‎ the Nun is central to his name. Jonah disobeys God and is thrown into the sea. He is swallowed by a fish נון‎ *Nun,* but instead of death he finds life and a renewed *faith* in God. Fish are noted for their fertility and were the first creatures to be blessed by God. "Be fruitful and multiply, and fill the waters in the seas."[255] Fish also make good fertilizer which helps crops to grow and become more abundant. Nun is related to the word for sprouting, flourishing and blossoming. Nun tells us that our faith will bring us into an abundant life.[256]

A fish is also at home when swimming amid the ebbing and flowing of the currents of the waters. The Nun reminds us that

---

[252] Scherman, pg. 151.
[253] Babylonian Talmud, Shabbath 104a.
[254] Hoffman, pg. 59.
[255] Genesis 1:22, KJV.
[256] John 10:10, KJV.

we too must feel at home amid the ebbing and flowing currents of life.

Yet, the fish remain cold and elusive. This is the warning or shadow of the Nun, to beware of being cold and allusive. In our quest for faithfulness we may shun and avoid those around us who may be hinder our faith. We dive under the waters to remain out of sight and end up in lonely waters. The Nun reminds us to beware of becoming cold and elusive and aloof.

The meanings behind the letter Nun are as follows:

Primary:

1. Emergence
2. Endurance
3. Faith and Faithfulness
4. An abundant life

Shadow:

1. Coldness
2. Aloofness

Samek ס

Samek is the fifteenth letter of the Hebrew Alphabet. It has a numerical value of sixty. The word *samek* סמך means *to rely on trust in, support, aid, assist, lay hands on, draw near, make close, encourage, or to be supported.* The word *samek* is used once in the Pentateuch, "And Joshua the son of Nun was full of the spirit of wisdom; for Moses had laid his hands upon him: and the children of Israel hearkened unto him, and did as the LORD commanded Moses."[257] Here the word *samek* is rendered in the KJV as *laid hands on*. To lay hands on something is to consider a form of consecration. Yet, the Hebrew word used for the laying on of hands has the idea of supporting. To lay hands on someone is to involve a spiritual anointing or support for that person. When I was ordained into the ministry all the local pastors from our denomination gathered around me and laid hands on me and prayed. In that they were committing themselves to support me in the ministry. The letter Samek is a letter of support.

The Talmud teaches that all acts done with the goal of Divine service, of becoming one with God, or of doing the will of God are acts that become endowed with a holiness whose physical manifestation is a support structure that functions to facilitate other such acts of holiness such as supporting the poor. [258] In other words the Samek is not only a call for spiritual support but to provide support in the natural world as well.

On September 10, 2001 David Wilkerson and his pastoral team were praying for spiritual support in the sanctuary of their church in Times Square, New York City. Suddenly they felt the call of God to beginning making sandwiches by the hundreds which they called their church together to do. The very next day was September 11, 2001 the day of the attack on the Twin Towers. In seeking spiritual support, David Wilkerson's church found they were ready to provide support on a natural level to those involved in the rescue operations. The Samek teaches that when we seek spiritual support we will be given the necessary tools to provide support on a natural level.

---

[257] Deuteronomy 34:9, KJV.
[258] Babylonian Talmud, Seder Moed, vol. 1, Shabbat, trans. H. Freeman (Soncino Press), 1938. pg. 500.

The word Samek has a numerical value of 120 (Samek = 60, Mem = 40, Kap = 20). Another word in the Hebrew that has numerical value of 120 is the word 'omed עומד which means *to stand*. It is used only once in the Pentateuch and that is when God speaks to Moses at the burning bush, "And he said, Draw not nigh hither: put off thy shoes from off thy feet, for the place whereon thou standest [is] holy ground."[259] So it is not so much the place he was standing on as the place he was supporting was holy ground. It was the position he was taking as one would say that they are *standing in favor* of something. Moses was standing before God totally in agreement with whatever God's plan was that He was going to share. The Samek is the opening letter for sod סוד which means *secret* or *hidden*. Before God even revealed his hidden plan to Moses he was already 'omed standing in support of God for God's plan. According to the sages, human existence is a mystery that ultimately only revelation, at certain times, can illumine. While in this world we do not consider or reflect on what it is we are *standing* upon. Each day as it passes we regard as though it has vanished into nothing, yet our words and deeds do live on.[260] The Samek reminds us that we all stand before God, but is our standing 'omed a standing in support of God's plan even though we cannot see his entire plan that is laid before us.

The shape of the Samek is like a o, or circle, it has an outer visible frame with an empty interior. There have been a significant amount of interpretations given for this. However, most agree that this is a symbol of God. He is entirely spiritual in nature without any physical form or characteristics as symbolized by the blank interior. The round closed frame of the Samek alludes to the whole earth which is filled with His glory so that wherever one is he can be in contact with the omnipresence of God.[261] Thus, the

[259] Exodus 3:5 KJV.
[260] Hoffman, pg. 62
[261] Scherman, pg. 160

very shape of the letter Samek tells us that God is supporting the entire world.

The Samek is not really a circle, the top of the Samek ס is flat although the cursive form in modern Hebrew makes it a circle. However, the flat top of the Samek is considered important to the sages for they say it is like a lid on a vessel or hut. It is a picture of a hiding place that you cover with a lid. The word sukkah סכה is related to the Samek and starts with the letter Samek.

The sukkah is a hut it is a shelter. The Samek reminds us that in God we can find a shelter and protection.[262]

The Samek is the number sixty. King Solomon had sixty body guards, valiant men who guarded him while he slept[263] These sixty body guards circled around Solomon at night to protect him from the terror of the nights. So too does the Samek ס, number sixty, remind us that God encircles us and surrounds us to protect us from the terrors of the dark. The Samek reminds us of God's protection.

Yet, despite all the protection and support that the Samek reminds us that we get from God, the Samek also reminds us of a warning, a shadow. The Samek is the letter of protection, but we can become overly guarded and defensive. We may be driven into seclusion to seek protection and thus shut ourselves out from the community that God may want to use to provide His protection for us.

The Samek also reminds us of another danger, the danger that we may become to supportive or too dependent upon other people. We can over extend and go beyond what is healthy for ourselves and others. An employer may work with a new employee, sharing his load, supporting him as he learns the trade, but there will come a time when that employee must learn to do the job himself, he must always keep in mind that the support he is

---

262 Seidman, pg. 110.
263 Song of Solomon 3:7-8.

getting is only temporary until he gets on his feet and is able to the job himself. The support of the Samek teaches us that support is simply a help, a push to get us over a difficult task, but we must always be mindful of what God has given us and to use that to the fullest.[264]

I can sum up the meaning of the Samek as follows:

Primary:

1. God supports us as we support others
2. Standing in support of God's plan even if we do not know the specifics of His plan.
3. God is supporting the entire world.
4. God's protection.

Shadow:

1. Shutting oneself out, becoming blocked off, and shut down.
2. Becoming either too supportive of or too dependent upon others.

Ayin ע

Ayin is the sixteenth letter of the Hebrew alphabet and has a numerical value of seventy. The word Ayin עין means *eye, sight sparkle and gleam.* We know there is something more than just an eye. An eye can reveal something inward about a person. We need to look someone in the eye to determine if they are truthful or not. It is by looking into someone's eyes that we gain insight into that person. The eye is the window through which character

---

[264] Seidman, pg. 115.

is discerned. David says that "my eyes are ever toward the Lord."
[265] What David is saying is that he is allowing God to look through
the window of his soul. He is saying that he is seeing God with his
intellect and intuition.[266] The Ayin is reminding us that God sees
our hearts not our outward appearance.[267]

The word Ayin עין also means *a spring or fountain*. A fountain
is a subterranean reservoir that feeds oceans and rivers.[268] This
brings out the idea of something that is deep and buried, as a
person's true character or intent is buried but is revealed through
his eyes. The Ayin is the letter of spiritual insight. The spring or
fountain also suggest a source. The eyes are a source of information into a person's consciousness.

The shape of the letter Ayin ע is like two eyes attached to a
pipe that faces leftward. On our left side is our heart. This shows
that our eyes our insight and consciousness will influence our
heart.[269] Thus we must set our eyes or our insight on what is
appropriate. In this way our heart can be purified, enabling us to
love God with all our heart. The sages teach that the two eyes on
the Ayin ע indicate that man has two eyes symbolically saying
that man has a free choice of what use to make of his eyes. Man
can condition himself to see the positive side of every situation or
the negative side. There is a story in the Talmud that when Rome
sacked Jerusalem and burned the temple some rabbis saw a fox
coming out of what was once the Holy of Holies and the rabbis
wept. On rabbi, however, laughed. They asked the rabbi why he
was laughing and the rabbi answered with a question, "Why do
you weep?" The rabbis replied because their sacred temple has

---

[265] Seidman, pg. 115.
[266] Finkel, Avraham Yaakov, The Great Chasidic Masters (Jason
Aronson), 1992, pg. 112.
[267] I Samuel 16:7.
[268] Haralick, pg. 230.
[269] Glazerson, Matityahu, Rabbi, Hebrew, The Source of Languages
(Yerid HaSafarim), 1987, pg. 79.

been so desecrated and destroyed that foxes now run in and out of the Holy place. The rabbi who was laughing replied, "Why that is exactly why I laugh for we have seen the fulfillment of Uriah's prophecy that Zion will be plowed like a field and Jerusalem shall become mounds of destruction (Micah 3:12, Jeremiah 26:18), surely we will now see the fulfillment of Zechariah's (8:4) prophecy that the streets of Jerusalem will be filled with boys and girls at play."[270]

The word Ayin is closely associated with the word aytsah עֵצָה which means advice. The Ayin teaches us that Spiritual development always involves the help of others. A Christian cannot stand alone. The Ayin encourages all believers to become part of a church or spiritual body. The Apostle Paul may have had the Ayin in mind when he said, "Not forsaking the assembling of ourselves together, as the manner of some [is]; but exhorting [one another]: and so much the more, as ye see the day approaching." [271] The Ayin is clearly teaching us to not forsake the assembling of yourselves with other believers. We need the advice, counsel, and encouragement from the body of believers to carry out God's plan.

The eye needs light to see so therefore the Ayin represents light and enlightenment. The Scripture tells us that where there is no vision, the people perish.[272] A seer is one who maintains a vision for his community and keeps that vision alive. The pastor of a church should be the Ayin of that church, the one who maintains the vision of that church, for without a vision the church will surely die. Many pastors lose their church because they have lost their vision for the church. The Ayin is the seer of the Hebrew Alphabet and this is reflected in its numerical value. Ayin equals seventy. Moses appointed seventy elders to be the *"eyes of the*

---

[270] Babylonian Talmud, Makkos 24.
[271] Hebrews 10:25, KJV.
[272] Proverbs 29:18 KJV.

community.[273] These seventy were granted the power of prophesy and in this they gained the perspective to judge wisely. The seventy elders became the model for the Sanhedrin, the highest religious court in Israel.

The Ayin calls us to pay attention to what we see. Often we just give a sweeping glance and do consider what we see. During my time in silence at the monastery I began to see things in trees, small animals, birds, the clouds and whatever else I could find of God's creation. I began to see things that I would normally not see during the rush of my normal life activities. I began to see God giving me a message and the song of dance of small birds, in the beauty of His sky I saw the message of His love and protection. The Ayin calls us to stop and look closely at God's creation for God does speak to us through His creation.

Yet, as we can learn and see things in God's creation through the encouragement of the Ayin, we must almost also heed Ayin's warning. The Talmud teaches, "The greater the sage, the greater the evil inclinations." Our brothers and sisters in the Catholic church are not alone in their sexual scandals. The church has been littered with abuses of power and sex found in many religious communities. The offenders are often men and women who sought to walk closely to God who sought out the light of the Ayin but forgot that as they approached the light there was shadow behind them. They became blind to their own dark sinful natures behind them. Even the great Apostle Paul wrestled with this dark side and declared that the thing he did not want to do he did.[274] The Ayin reminds us that we still have a sinful nature and although we have been cleansed through the Blood of Jesus Christ that does not mean that the old nature will not rear its ugly head at times when we seem to be so close to God. The light of God is not meant to blind us to our sin, but to reveal it to us.

[273] Numbers 11:24-25.
[274] Romans 7:15, KJV.

The Ayin reminds us that our eyes may not always see what is of God. The Ayin is also a symbol of coveting and greed. "The eyes of man are never satisfied."[275] The Ayin is there to remind us to be aware of what our eyes see and to cultivate an inner seeing that does not grasp for satisfaction outside oneself.

The meaning of the Ayin can be expressed in the following words:

Primary:

1. Perception and Insight
2. We can see things two ways, positive or negative
3. We are not to forsake the assembling of believers
4. Light and enlightenment
5. Pay close attention to what you see in God's creation.

Shadow:

1. Beware of the darkness hidden in the shadow behind you.
2. Coveting and greed.

Pei פ

Pei is the seventeenth letter in the Hebrew Alphabet. Pei has a numerical value of eighty. The final form of Pei ף has a numerical value of eight hundred. Pei may be spelled either פא or פה . The word Pei פה means *mouth, speech, saying, command, opening, entrance, extremity or border.* Pei carries the idea of a passage way for speech or into a territory. Everything that happens physically, mentally, emotionally or spiritually can be transformed into action

---

[275] Proverbs 27:20, KJV.

only after passing through the border or entranceway into our existence which is either verbally or nonverbally. In many places in the Bible the word Pei is render as *here*. Each time it is used it is used to express a place where significant things are about to happen. The mouth is an entrance or opening to action. Hence we see the meaning of the Pei to be not only a mouth but a point where something significant is about to happen.[276]

The mouth makes it possible to fulfill the ultimate purpose of creation, to sing praises to God and study His Word. David teaches that the dead do not praise God.[277] However, living people who have a physical mouth can praise God by virtue of their speech.

The Talmud teaches that the Pei directs us in the use of our mouths. The Pei takes two forms. When it appears at the beginning or middle of a word it is expressed as פ but when it appears at the end of a word it is in its final form ף. The Talmud alludes to two different functions of the mouth, open פ and closed ף. The teaching is that the mouth should sometimes be open and it should sometimes be closed.[278] The mouth should be open to teach, and there is a time for the mouth to be closed so as not to compete. I have attended many Sunday School classes and Bible studies where some have tried to out teach the teacher. They feel they have a great grasp of a passage of Scripture and feel it is their duty to enlighten the others. Perhaps their contribution is worthy, but if done at the wrong time with the wrong intent, they will only foster conflict and ill will. The Talmud instructs us to not compete with those who teach. Far too often someone's contribution is meant to compete with the teacher and the result is much ill will and embarrassment. In the process the Holy Spirit is grieved and if the Holy Spirit is our ultimate teacher, then when He is

---

[276] Haralick, pg. 245.
[277] Psalms 115:17, KJV.
[278] Babylonian Talmud, Shabbat 104a.

grieved into silence there is no longer any teaching. The Pei not only instructs us to speak, but also to keep silent. The Talmud teaches that to shame a person in public is akin to murder.[279]

The Pei begins the word *poht* for *opening* and *patach* for *doorway*. This symbolizes that our speech has the power to open doorways. The Pei reminds us of the tremendous force inherent in human communication.[280]

Inspired speech is Pei's ideal. We learn from Scripture that the heart of the wise teaches is one's mouth (Pei).[281] God speaks to our hearts, when our hearts are joined to the heart of God we speak God's heart. Far too many pastors preach from books, lexicons and commentaries. They will spend hours researching their sermons and preach from their minds. This is all well and good and pastors should spend considerable time studying the Word of God, but when he speaks, he must speak from his heart and not his mind. He must live every sermon that he preaches. The Pei instructs us that when we teach we must teach from the heart.

The shadow of the Pei is very obvious. Sometimes we speak too much. Many of us open our mouths without giving thought to what is going to come out and then we regret it later. The Pei is calling us to consider what we say very careful and not to speak too much.

On the other hand we may be too quiet. The Pei calls us to a balanced communication. Someone we know may desperately need a kind word spoke or a misunderstanding must be cleared up, but we hesitate to speak out. We may witness a crime and out of fear keep quiet. The Pei is calling us to action to speak out when the occasion calls for it.

Of course the Pei has a lot to say about gossip. Putting people down and spreading rumors is very human. Pei is quietly asking

---

[279] Hoffman. 'pg. 68.
[280] Ibid., pg. 69.
[281] Proverbs 16:23, KJV.

us to resist this temptation and instead to use uplifting speech, to offer words of blessing and not cursing.[282]

The summary of the meaning for the Pei is as follows:

Primary:

1. Mouth, communication
2. A point where something significant is about to happen
3. Speaking out, expressing your inner self
4. Keeping silent
5. Speech is a very powerful tool
6. Speak from the Heart.

Shadow:

1. Talking too much
2. Not talking enough
3. Gossiping

Sade צ

The Sade is the eighteenth letter of the Hebrew Alphabet. It has a numerical value of ninety. It has a final form ץ which carries a numerical value of nine hundred. The word Sade comes from a root form צד which means to capture. The Sade צ looks like someone who is kneeling or bowed down either in surrender as a captive or in humility. When one has been captured, he has surrendered and he is humbled. Hence the basic meaning of the letter Sade is humility. The word Sade also forms the word tsadiq צדיק which means *righteousness, honesty, uprightness, pious and correct.* This is summed up in the

---

[282] Seidman, pg. 129.

word *righteous.* Sade is a powerful word calling us to humility and righteousness.

There are two forms of the letter Sade. There is the bent Sade c which is used when beginning a word or in the middle of a word and there is the Final form of the Sade ץ which is used at the end of word. This is known in the Talmud as the bent Sade and the erect Sade.[283] The bent Sade is God reaching down to man in His righteousness and the erect Sade is a righteous man reaching up to God. Somewhere in between should be the angels, they are also called righteous. However, the angels will automatically carry out God's will, but a human is greater than angel as he serves God of his own free will.[284] The Sade speaks not only of the righteousness of God but of a man as well.

The final form of the Sade ץ denotes the righteous person in the world to come as opposed to the righteous person in the present world צ. The righteous person in this world is continually on his knees, but in heaven he will be erect as he will stand in the very presence of God.[285]

The letter Sade as the word Sade is built into the word for charity צדקה Tsadakah. The Sade reminds us to aid the poor and less fortunate not for philanthropic sentiment, but because it is a vital act of justice.[286]

Jewish tradition teaches that in every generation there are the Lamed -Vavs (36) *Tsaddikim* לו צדיקים Thirty six Righteous Ones. These Thirty six hold the world together with their goodness and virtuous acts. These thirty six righteous ones are hidden and living humbly and performing in secret their wonderful and miraculous deeds. Sometimes they are disguised as rough

---

[283] Babylonian Talmud, Shabbat 104a.
[284] Metsudah Midrash Tanchuman Bereishis 5 (Metsudah Publications), 2005.
[285] Babylonian Talmud, Shabbat 104a.
[286] Hoffman, pg. 72.

hoodlum biker's type, sometimes as a homeless beggar or someone who is mentally challenged, but always the intention of the
tzaddik is to uplift and unify. The Sade calls us to be alert to their
presence and show respect to all regardless of their race, religion,
or character, for without them the world would collapse. In other
words the Sade is calling us to look for the best in people.

I recall as a young child my father helped to establish a rescue
mission in Chicago. I would go downtown to the skid row area
of Chicago every Wednesday where my father would preach to
these men off the streets and I would play the piano. One day one
of the men from the streets walked up to me. I was just a little
eleven year old child. This man was ragged, he smelled of whisky,
his hair was wild and matted, he had a four day old beard, his eyes
were blood shot, his face marked and wrinkled, and his nose was
bright red. He walked up to me and said: "Son, look at me." I did.
He then asked, "Am I pretty?" I shook my head no and then he
said, "That's what whiskey will do to you." Then he walked away. I
have sat under many teachers in my day, some of the best teachers in the evangelical world, but this man was probably the best
teacher I ever had. I was never, ever even tempted to take a drink,
always remembering what this man, maybe one of the Thirty Six,
told me. Of course there are no Thirty Six righteous who hold the
world together with their righteousness, but the legend, as the
Sade reminds us, is that a righteous person can appear from some
of the most unexpected places. Indeed this man off the streets of
skid row in Chicago performed a righteous act that changed my
life. The Sade whispers to us that even the worst of us, when they
fall on their knees in humility before the Savior Jesus Christ, they
too can become righteous and perform righteous acts.

As pious as the Sade is with all its righteousness, there is a
shadow. The shadow of the Sade of course is self-righteousness.
The Sade צ is formed by the letter Nun נ leaning down toward the

left with the Yod ' resting on top of it, the rabbis of old have taught that the Sade represents the act of bowing down in humility. The Sade reminds us that humility can temper the tendency toward getting puffed up with self-righteousness.[287]

This leads to another warning from the Sade and that is trying to live up to unrealistic standards then expecting others to live up to the same standard and being critical of those who do not.[288] As the old Quaker once said, "There are only two people in this world who are living the perfect life, me and thee, but sometimes I wonder about thee."

I remember when I was a student at Moody Bible Institute we had another student who started to go to a church that carried very high standards of conduct, higher than those of Moody. Initially this student worked very hard to live up to those standards and we could see him failing in many areas, but since we were no better, we never said anything. Before long this student started to condemn us and criticize us every time we failed to live up to the standards of *righteousness* that his church taught. Before long he found he did not have many friends and so left Moody saying that we were all, for want of a better word, sinners. That is exactly what the Sade wants to remind us of, we are all sinners who are saved by the grace of God through Jesus Christ.

I would sum of the meaning behind the letter Sade to be:

Primary:

1. Humility
2. Righteousness of God
3. The righteousness of man made possible through Jesus Christ
4. Charity

---

[287] Seidman, pg. 137.
[288] Ibid.

Shadow:

1. Self-righteousness
2. Condemning others for not living up to unrealistically high standards

Qop ק

The Qop ק is the nineteenth letter of the Hebrew Alphabet and has a numerical value of one hundred. Qop is the letter with alludes to God's holiness.[289] The term *holiness of God* conveys the message that He is supremely exalted. He is unlimited; his is neither obligated nor related to anything existing. He has no resemblance to anything or anyone. He is boundless and formless, His spirit penetrates the entire universe.[290]

The concept of holiness implies that the thing that is under discussion is removed from other matters. If an object is holy then it has a degree of sanctity about it that forbids its used for ordinary pleasures. If a person is considered holy it is implied that he is on a higher level than others. God is holy in the sense that no being, whether human or spiritual can compare to Him.[291]

The word Qop קף has a numerical value of 186 (Qop = 100, Vav = 6, Pei = 80). Another word in Hebrew that has a value of 186 is the word *maqom* מקם. This word means *omnipresent*. This is one of the Divine names of God, it is one aspect that makes God holy for no other being can be *omnipresent*. The Qof ק is constructed with the letter Vav ו and Kap כ. The Kap has a numerical value of twenty and the Vav has a numerical value of six giving a total value of twenty six. The name of God YHWH יהוה has a numerical value of twenty six (Yod = 10, Hei = 5, Vav = 6, Hei = 5). The

---

[289] Babylonian Talmud, Shabbat, 104a.
[290] Scherman, pg. 194.
[291] I0062id.

very construction of the Qop indicates that it is related to God and His holiness.

Yet, if holiness belongs to God then how can it be demanded of man, "Ye shall be holy: for I the LORD your God [am] holy." [292] Man's holiness is shown by placing all his instincts and inclinations at the disposal of God's will. Man can only accomplish this through Jesus Christ who commanded it.[293]

The word Qop קוף means *monkey or ape*. The sages explain that God created the ape as an inferior image of man to remind man that because of sin we can never reach that perfect state that God created man to be. Although the monkey resembles man more than any other animal does, it can never reach the level of the human being. Just as man may resemble that perfect man that God created, sin and his sinful nature makes it impossible for him to reach that state of perfection. Only through Jesus Christ will man one day when freed from this sinful body be able to enter into that perfect state. The Qop reminds us that as the monkey is to man in the natural world, so is the human man to his future spiritual state in the world to come.[294]

Qop is related to the Hebrew word korban קרבן which means *sacrifice*. The Qop reminds us that holiness is only achieved through the sacrifice of the things of this world. Holiness is setting ourselves apart from this world. The Apostle Paul teaches that we are not to be conformed to this world but to be transformed.[295] This means sacrificing many of the things of this world that are not in harmony with God to bring us into a harmony with Him.[296]

Qop has the numerical value of one hundred. One hundred has been traditional accepted as the number of completion and

---

[292] Leviticus 19:2, KJV.
[293] I Peter 1:16, KJV.
[294] Babylonian Talmud, Sanhedrin 109a
[295] Romans 12:2, KJV.
[296] Hoffman, pg. 76.

perfection. The word *holy* is related to the word *whole*. When a cycle is complete holiness or wholeness is fulfilled. Ending often signifies a death.[297] Life is a cycle, we are born, live and die. When that cycle is complete, the Oop reminds us that we are then made whole, we are made whole through the Qop, the sacrifice, of Jesus Christ as we enter our eternal state in heaven, made whole and perfect having accepted the gift of salvation through Jesus Christ.

The Qop like the other letters also gives us a warning or shadow. The Qop warns us that in our quest to become holy we can project our unholiness, our insecurities and weaknesses on others. I once had a roommate in college who boasted that he had not committed any sins for over three years. Of course being his roommate, if we did not get along, you can guess whose fault it was.

The Qop is there to take our hand in our quest to be holy before God reminding us that we do have a sinful nature and it will be with us until we enter our final state. The Qop is there to remind us that we are prone to failure and sinfulness and to always take responsibility for our actions and not blame it on others.

The meanings behind the Qop can be listed as follows:

Primary:

1. Holiness
2. Completion and wholeness
3. Man can only become holy through Jesus Christ
4. Sacrifice
5. We are made holy and complete through the sacrifice of Jesus Christ.

---

[297] Seidman, pg. 139.

Shadow:

1. Bringing shame on condemnation unto others
2. Not taking responsibility for one's own sinful actions.
3. Even though we are a new creation through Jesus Christ, we still have a sinful nature until we complete this cycle in life and are one with Jesus in our eternal state.

Resh ר

The Resh is the twentieth letter of the Hebrew Alphabet. It has a numerical value of two hundred. The word Resh רֵישׁ is identical to the word Rosh רֹאשׁ which means *head, leader, principal, commander, ruler or prince*. It has the idea of headship or leadership. We do not find Resh רֵישׁ in the Pentateuch but we do find permutation of this word in *sari* שָׂרִי. This is where the name of Sarai (Sarah), the name of Abraham's wife is built by adding a Hei ה to sari putting it into a feminine form. Although Abraham is the father of the Hebrew race, Sarah is also the head or mother of the Hebrew race.[298]

The Talmud asks the question, "Why is the face of the Qop ק turned away from the Resh ר? Actually the face of the Qop ק does not turn away from the Resh ר but stands behind the Resh. The Resh is the *rasha'* רָשָׁע the wicked and the holiness of God, the Qop ק cannot stand to look upon the wickedness. Yet it stands behind the Resh ready to receive it in repentance.[299] The Resh stands for repentance. In fact the shape of the Resh ר teaches us what repentance truly is. The Resh ר is like a path that makes a sudden turn. Repentance is turning away from the path you were following to follow a new path toward the Qop ק or holiness. You will remember that the Qop also represents sacrifice. Our

---

[298] Haralick, pg. 283-284.
[299] Babylonian Talmud, Shabbat 104a.

repentance will not lead us to holiness without the sacrifice and the shedding of the blood of the lamb, our Lamb Jesus Christ.

The Resh begins the words for *ruach hakadosh* רוח הקדש which means the Holy Spirit.[300] It is also the word for wind. Jesus said the Spirit of God is like the wind, you cannot see it nor know where it comes.[301] The Holy Spirit is our head, our leader, our guide, the one who leads us into all truth. Thus, the Resh reminds us of the work of the Holy Spirit in our lives.

The word Resh ריש also mean spiritual poverty and moral emptiness. The Resh reminds us of our moral emptiness and our need for repentance, turning to the Holiness of God and relying on the Holy Spirit as our guide and teacher to holiness.[302]

The Resh represents leadership and thus comes with a warning toward those who accept a leadership role. The shadow of the Resh teaches us that when we accept a leadership role we face a temptation to abuse that role. Leadership can easily veer toward egotism, arrogance and corruption. The Resh reminds us to always be vigilant and on guard against these sometimes subtle tendencies.[303]

The Resh cries out to those in leadership roles to acknowledge their tendencies toward this abuse and to repent of these abuses immediate, turn away from them and move into the direction of the Qop, holiness. The shadow of the Resh reminds us of the abuse of leadership and power.

The Resh also casts another shadow. When we do repent and move toward the Qop of holiness we forget that we do have a sinful nature. As we seek to live a righteous and holy life we can become judgmental and condemning of those who do not live such a life. Resh does not shy away from naming sins, but the

---

[300] Hoffman, pg. 77
[301] John 3:8. KJV.
[302] Seidman, pg. 145-146.
[303] Seidman, pg. 145-146.

Resh is also the first letter to Rachamim רחמים which is compassion and mercy. When we do see others who are not living a holy life the Resh calls out to us to not condemn them for what we are prone to ourselves, but to have compassion and identify when a wrong is harmful. When we veer off into self-righteousness and being judgmental we have entered the shadow of the Resh.[304]

The meanings behind the Resh are represented as:

Primary:

1. Leadership, headship
2. Repentance
3. Holy Spirit

Shadow:

1. Self-righteousness and being judgmental
2. Abuse of leadership

Shin ש

The Shin is the twenty-first letter of the Hebrew alphabet. The word Shin שן means urine and if you drop the Yod in Shin you have Sen שן which means to chew, tooth or jaw. This tells us that the Shin represents a totality of an overall process from eating, to digestion to the elimination of the waste. Thus, the Shin has the meaning of *whole entire, intact, or complete.* Also such an overall process needs to be repeated over and over. Shin is related to the word שנה shanah which means to repeat over and over. When coupled with the Resh, the prior letter you have שנה ראש Rosh Shanah which means the top of the year or the New

---

[304] Ibid, pg. 148.

Year. Again the idea of repeating or doing again or returning. The Shin reminds us that when we wander too far away from God, He is always waiting for our return.

There is the story in the Talmud about a king who had a disagreement with his son. The disagreement was such that the son left home to live in another kingdom. After some time the king, the father, sent a messenger to the son with the message, "Please come home." The son replied that it was too far for him to come. The father sent the messenger back with another message, "Then come as far as you can and I will meet you." Jesus retold this story in the form of the prodigal son, only in the version Jesus told, when the father met his son he hugged and kissed him. The Shin is reminding us to return home to God, to come as far as we can and He will meet us with a hug and kiss.

The letter Shin שׁ is shaped with a base that has three arms extending upward. Jewish tradition teaches that the right arm of the Shin שׁ is a Yod י which teaches that we receive wisdom from heaven, the left side is a Zayin ז which teaches that from the left side there flows a weapon of defense to bring peace and the center of the Shin שׁ is the Vav ו which connects us with heaven. Thus the Shin brings the Zayin ז, Vav ו and Yod י into balance and harmony. The Shin teaches us that the peace of the Zayin, the wisdom of God and the connection with heaven will bring us into harmony with God. The Shin reminds us that we can enjoy a harmony with God through the peace and wisdom of God.[305]

The left arm of the Shin represents the Zayin which is a weapon to bring peace. The Shin is the first letter in the word shalom שׁלם which means *peace*. Shalom has a wide range of meanings, not just an absence of strife, but the presence of wholeness and prosperity. Shin speaks to us of peace and harmony.[306]

---

[305] Glazerson, Matityahu Rabbi, From Hinduism to Judaism (Himselsein Publishers), 1984, pg. 83.
[306] Hoffman, pg. 80.

The Shin is the letter of אֵשׁ *ish* which is the word for fire. The three upraised arms are flames of holy fire. The word for sun in Hebrew is Shemesh שֶׁמֶשׁ which begins and ends with a Shin. The Shin kindles a fire Sh'viv שָׁבִיב, the Shin brings heat sharav שָׁרָב . The shin is also the flame of the fire shalhevet שַׁלְהֶבֶת. The Shin represents the kindling, flame and heat of a fire a fire is considered a passion, a fiery passion and thus the Shin reminds us of the fiery passion of God.

Fire reminds us of so much, we think of the destructiveness of fire, the cleansing of fire, the beauty of fire, the colors of fire. God appeared to Moses in a burning bush to symbolize his passionate love for His people.

Yet fire has it's down side, its shadow. We speak of fiery anger, the fires of lust or the fires of jealousy. The Shin reminds us to beware of these fires, to be alert for a spark anger, lust or jealousy and not to fan the spark into a flame where it will become destructive. One must be careful with fire, it can be used to light a home, provide heat, and cook food, but it can also burn a house to the ground. The shin calls to us to treat fire with respect so to with the passion of God. When God opens up his fiery passion to us, He is making Himself vulnerable as we do when we open up our loving passion to another person. Many have been deeply hurt when that one we share our passionate love with betrays that love, betrays that fiery passion. The greater the blaze of passion the greater the heartbreak when it is betrayed. Being made in the image of God means that we share His passions and heartbreak. As God shares His passion with us, He has made Himself vulnerable to us, He has given us the ability to deeply wound His heart when we betray His love for other Gods. The Shin cries out to us in a blaze of passion to treat the heart and love of God with the respect that a devoted husband would treat the heart of his wife. The Shin is one of the most commonly used letters in the Alphabet, it is used continually to be a continual reminder to respect the heart of God.[307]

We can summarize the meanings behind the Shin as follows:

Primary:

1.   Wholeness, completeness
2.   God is waiting for our return to Him.
3.   Harmony with God
4.   Peace and harmony with God
5.   Protecting the heart of God

Shadow:

Being consumed by anger, lust and jealousy

Taw ת

The Taw ת is the twenty-second letter of the Alphabet and has a numerical value of 400. The word Taw ת means mark, sign, line feature, musical note or label. A sign is that by which something is made known. A sign is something that can be externally recognized and which signals something internal. In other words a sign is a distinctive and uniquely recognizable covering that signifies and internal essence. For instance we see a sign that says, danger. It is signifying something that may not be visible to use at that moment but will be a danger when it is recognized. A sign is telling us a truth, we can recognize the truth by its signs. Thus the Taw represents truth. The Taw is the seal of the truth.[308]

---

[307] Seidman, pg. 152-158.
[308] Babylonian Talmud, Shabbat 55a.

The word Taw תו has a numerical value of 406 (Taw = 400, Vav = 6). Another word in Hebrew that also has a value of 406 is baqodesh בקדש (Beth = 2, Qop = 100, Daleth = 4, Shin = 300). Baqodesh means in holiness as the Scripture records, "Who [is] like unto thee, O LORD, among the gods? who [is] like thee, glorious in holiness, fearful [in] praises, doing wonders?" [309] Truth is found in the Holiness of God. Holiness is the sign or mark of God which is expressed in truth.

The Talmud teaches that the letters Shin ש and Taw ת are neighbors in the Alphabet, they are worlds apart. For the Shin begins the word for falsehood, shaqar שקר while the Taw begins the word for truth 'emet. אמת.[310] However, truth must not have even the hint of falsehood, even a trifle turns truth into falsehood. For even with if you remove the smallest of the numerical value the Aleph א from the word truth אמת what remains is moth מת which means death. The Talmud teaches to tell the truth is so important because if you are caught in a lie then even when you tell the truth it will not be believed.[311]

Truth is symbolized in the Taw since the power of truth lies in its results. The Talmud teaches that the Divine judicial pronouncement that was used when God decreed the destruction of Jerusalem and ordered the angel Gabriel, as seen in the vision of Ezekiel chapter 9, to put a mark (Hebrew - Taw ת) on the foreheads of the citizens of Jerusalem To differentiate the righteous ones destined for life in the World to Come from the wicked who were doomed to perish in this world and the next, ink and blood were used respectively. A ת Taw in ink was placed on the forehead of the righteous, denoting תחיה "you shall live" and in blood for the wicked a ת Taw denoting תמות "you shall die."[312] The Taw is a

[309] praises, doing wonders
[310] Babylonian Talmud, Shabbat 104a.
[311] Babylonian Talmud, Sanhedrin 89.
[312] Ibid., Shabbat 55a

strong letter a sign and mark denoting truth which will separate and remove any falsehood.

Truth is perfection. The Taw teaches us of perfection, the last letter of the Alphabet cries out Divine perfection, God is perfect. "[As for] God, his way [is] perfect:"[313] The Taw is instructing us of Divine perfection.

This Divine perfection which ends the Hebrew Alphabet encourages by reminding us that in the end through Jesus Christ we will be *tiqun* תקן which means redeemed. Tiqun is spelled Taw - redemption, Qop - Sacrifice and Nun - faith. Using the esoteric language of the ancient rabbis we learn that redemption the Taw takes place through the sacrifice of Jesus Christ the Qop and we received this redemption through the Nun - faith.

Taw begins the word for *prayer* תפללה *talilpah.*[314] We received this redemption through prayer. But now that we have been through the entire Hebrew Alphabet with its meanings, let us look at this word for prayer as it will reveal just what type of prayer will bring redemption. This is a prayer that is prayed with a Taw ת - truth, it is spoken with the Pei פ, truth with two Lameds לל representing uplifted hands. The first Lamed ל taking our confession from our heart and lifting it up to heaven and the second Lamed ל receiving something from heaven into our hearts. What do we receive? Well we asked for the Taw ת - redemption which will receive but we will also receive the Hei ה, the presence of God into our lives. As the Apostle Paul said, "For with the heart man believeth unto righteousness; and with the mouth confession is made unto salvation."[315]

The Taw as the last letter of the Alphabet leaves us with a shadow, warning about endings. Sometimes we bring an ending about prematurely, we are praying and trusting God and it seems

---

[313] Psalms 18:30, KJV.
[314] Hoffman, pg. 85.
[315] Romans 10:10, KJV.

there is no answer and before long we give up, we bring our prayers to an end. The Taw is warning us against a premature ending, just as the Taw is the natural end of the alphabet our prayers will reach a natural end, relationships will reach a natural end, ministries will reach a natural end, we must beware of ending before the time that God has designated.[316]

On the other hand, there is the warning of not ending something when it should end. Sometimes there are relationships that should end especially when they become detrimental to our relationship with God.[317] There are ministries that should end and be replaced with something new and fresh. I recall when took the pastorate of a new church. The first group I was asked to speak to in the church was the YMPC. I found that the youngest person in the class was seventy eight years old. When I asked what YMPC stood for I was told, Young Married Person's Class. Somehow they never got around to changing their name after all the years they were organized. Well, there was no real harm here and my suggestion to change their name to something like the Homeward Bound Class just did not set well so they remained YMPC until the very end. However, this church also had a children's program that was dying out, a day camp program where they could get no volunteers, but somehow they felt that this had to continue and any suggestion that they just close down the program and bring in something new to replace it met with great resistance. Yet, times change and approaches must change with them. I worked for a number of years for an organization known as Campus Life, previously known as Youth for Christ. They were continually on the cutting edge so to speak because their motto was, "Geared to the times, but anchored to the Rock."

---

[316] Seidman, pg. 164
[317] Ibid.

The Taw is calling us to recognize when something has run its course and it is ready to end and be replaced, to be geared to the times but always anchored to the Rock.

We can summarize the meanings behind the Taw with the following:

Primary:

1. Mark, sign
2. Truth
3. Divine perfection
4. Redemption

Shadow:

1. Ending relationships and situations prematurely
2. Clinging to relationships and situations beyond a healthy endpoint.

The Mystery Letter

There is a belief among the mystic Jews that there is one letter missing from the current Alphabet. Every defect in our present world stems from the absence of this letter. When this letter is revealed then all defect will disappear. The missing consonant sound is unimaginable, inconceivable and will combine all the letters to create new words and new worlds. All will become complete with this letter.

The Talmud teaches that this letter appeared on the original set of tablets which the Ten Commandments were inscribed. When the tablets were broken because of the sin of the Israelites all the letters flew off the tablets and ascended to Heaven. The letters eventually returned, but the twenty-third letter had vanished from this world.

Jewish mystics speculate that this missing letter is a four pronged Shin. You will find a four pronged Shin on the left side of the tefillin, the small black box worn on the head during morning prayers. The left side commemorates the missing letter. The missing letter promises a better future but its shadow reminds us to not abandon the present.[318]

As a Christian it is only fitting that the Hebrew Alphabet ends with this mysterious letter which we, of course, will believe to be Jesus Christ Himself.

---

[318] Seidman, pg. 165-167. ;

Chapter Three
THE GEMETRIA

What is the Gematria

The ancient Jewish teachers believed that words were creeds, beliefs couched in the code of letters merged so as to have meaning on many levels. When studying Jewish literature such as the Talmud and Mishnah I was surprised at the farfetched inferences, allusions and even numerical correspondences that were suggested to be credible explications. Yet, we do some of the same with our English language. For instance we have acronyms. For instance the word *radar* is a very common word used in our language and if you take a survey of a hundred people most if not all could tell you how radar is used. Yet if you ask the same people what the letters of the word *radar r-a-d-a-r* means only a handful if any could tell you. In fact most would be surprised to learn that it is an acronym standing for *R*adio *D*etecting *A*nd *R*anging. To someone learning the English language to try and explain that radar can be related to a longer phrase of four words, would seem farfetched to them.

We stop at a restaurant and ask for a *Coke* and the waitress makes the annoying correction that they only serve Pepsi or RC. What we really mean is a cola type beverage but the word Coke has so been associated with a cola beverage that we used the trade name to describe a cola beverage. The English language is a very difficult language to understand and learn with all our many idioms and colloquialisms. Someone just learning the English language would be confused at an American being satisfied in having to order a Coke and ending up with a Pepsi. Then too, few people never stop to explore the word Coke and its origins. Again if you were to ask the same one hundred people where the name Coke came from, few would know that originally Coke Cola contained cocaine. Perhaps three thousand years from now after the English language becomes a dead language some lexicographer might write in an English Lexicon that Coke Cola was a beverage containing cocaine which people in the twentieth and twenty first century used to stimulate themselves. Depending on how buried the English language becomes in three thousand years this lexicographer may entirely overlook the fact that cocaine was no longer used in Coke Cola after the nineteenth century. So three thousand years from now history teachers may be teaching their students that twentieth and twenty first century man regularly got high drinking something called Coke Cola and that they believed a similar beverage called Pepsi gave them new vigor because of the word *Pep* in Pepsi. With so many other stimulants around few people actually consciously drink a cola beverage as a stimulant more than just a preferred tasting substitute for water to quench one's thirst.

By all this I am not suggesting that the esoteric structure of the Hebrew Alphabet is a perfect tool to be used in one's personal Bible study, I am only saying that it is something worth exploring and if fitting the pieces of the esoteric use of the language provides an incentive to study the Word of God, in just that it has proven some value.

I, personally, will spend three to four hours a day studying one verse in the Bible, playing around with the meanings behind letters and the Gematria as purely a form of entertainment. However, in the end I have found that I spent three to four hours meditating on one verse of the Bible. Whether the Gemetria and meanings behind the letters have added anything new to my original understanding of the verse is often debatable, but what is certain is that the esoteric structure of the Hebrew Alphabet has motivated me to study that verse in a depth I would not normally study a passage of Scripture.

One of the most intriguing and perhaps the one often least acceptable to the Western mind, simply because of unfamiliarity is the code of Gematria. This must not be associated with Numerology which has a mystical element to it. In a way it is almost like a game where you note the fact that two totally different words, when translated into the language of numbers (every Hebrew letter also bears a numerical equivalent) share the same total and hence you seek to find a relationship between the two.

Let's say I am studying the passage of Scripture in II Kings 8:11: "And the man of God wept." I may pause here and think of John 11:35: "Jesus wept." I am intrigued by the fact that Elijah a man of God wept and Jesus Himself wept. I would like to meditate on this, so what I would do is look at the Hebrew word for *weeping* which is *beki* בְּכִי. I look into my lexicon and discover that this word has its origins in the picture of dropping or dripping of water as in tears flowing from one's eyes.[319] What made Elijah and Jesus weep was the knowledge of what was going to befall God's people.[320] So what is this strange power behind weeping? Looking at the form of the word *weep* or *cry* as used in this passage I find it is *beki*. This is spelled Beth - 2, Kap - 20 and Yod - 10 which equals 32. I then consider other words which have a similar numerical value. I find that the numerical value for the word *heart* לֵב is Lamed - 30, Beth - 2 also has a numerical value of 32. Since words with the same numerical value in Hebrew are in some way related, I will meditate on this and I would personally conclude that *weeping comes from the heart.* When we speak to God we

---

[319] Davidson, pg. 83.
[320] II Kings 8, KJV.

know that the words which come from the heart are the words that are most acceptable to the Almighty. Thus, many times when we pray we may find ourselves weeping because the words we are expressing to God are coming from our heart. David Wilkerson remarked that he was always amazed that the touch of the Holy Spirit expresses itself in tears.[321] Weeping has it source, not from the lips but from the heart. We even use the expression, *crying our hearts out*. Shakespeare expressed it well when he said, "I will wear him in my heart's core, in my *heart of heart*."[322] We all have a special place in our hearts, the core of our hearts or heart of heart that we guard very closely. If anyone or anything penetrates to the core, it will result in weeping.

"Godly sorrow works repentance."[323] True repentance many times comes with weeping for true repentance flows from the heart's core, our heart of hearts. True prayer comes from the heart's core, our heart of hearts. We guard that core of our hearts so well because we know that even the slightest breeze outside its protective cover will wound it.

How difficult it is to expose our heart's core, our heart of hearts to anyone, even to God. So it is with God. He will not expose us to that core of His heart, His heart of hearts unless he can really trust us not to wound His heart. Do we really want to enter the core of God's heart, His heart of hearts? If we do will we feel His grief, the grief that Jesus feels. For the sorrow that Jesus observed touch His heart, we know that because he wept.[324] Could this be what the Apostle Paul meant when he said that as heirs of God and joint heirs of Christ we suffer with Him?[325] When we weep for the sin and suffering of this world, could it be that the tears we

---

[321] Wilkerson, David, The Cross and the Switchblade (Pyramid Publications), 1977., pg. 148.
[322] Hamlet Act 3 Scene 2
[323] II Corinthians 7:10, KJV.
[324] John 11:35, KJV.
[325] Romans 8:17, KJV.

shed are from the pain that we feel from God' s heart, His sorrow and His heartbreak over a lost world? Perhaps this is why Elijah wept in II Kings 8:11, he was not weeping from his own wounded heart over the sin of the nation but he was weeping with God as his heart was joined with God.

I have just taken you on a little journey through one passage of scripture with just one word, *weep,* and came upon a discovery which is something that I would find personally edifying in my walk with God. I would certainly not teach this as any truth, doctrine or dogma, it is just a personal observation which I will carry within my own heart. It in no way conflicts with my orthodox beliefs, it is certainly no new revelation for the church, I am sure millions of other Christians have shared the same thoughts. Yet, I came upon this by using the Gematria as a tool.

I believe few people would argue the fact that weeping comes from the heart. What many may find disturbing is to say that this was the intended reason for the Hebrew words for heart and weeping to have the same numerical value. Perhaps it is just a pleasant little coincidence, or perhaps God designed the Hebrew language this way to give each word its own personal commentary. We can never be sure but one thing we do know, there are hundreds, if not thousands of such coincidences that have been discovered and that alone should make the occasional use of the Gematria worthwhile. Haim Shore, an engineering professor in Israel, in fact, wrote a three hundred page book documenting hundreds of such coincidences.[326]

The Gematria has evolved over many generations of Jewish mysticism and beyond. The art of Gematria has been integrated into numerous Jewish books of scholarship and interpretations of Scriptural texts, and it is considered to this day an acceptable and

---

[326] Shore, Haim Coincidences in the Bible and in the Biblical Hebrew, (I Universe, Inc.), 2012.

legitimate practice in all denominations of the Jewish faith.[327] As the Jewish people are the guardians of the ancient Hebrew language and the people of the language, I would consider their insights to be of great value. For many of the orthodox Jewish faith the Gematria is not a matter of coincidences but an actual linguistical tool and a design by God. According to this view the Gematria logic was created through God's utterances. Each letter in the Hebrew alphabet represents a different creative force. Since the letter carries a numerical value, the numerical equivalence of two words reveals an internal connection between the creative potential of each one. Therefore the study of words with equal numerical values may lead one to the common concept that binds the words together, thus delivering an insight into the meaning of this shared concept.[328]

Whether by design of God or coincidence is a question that is left open for the sake of this paper. The purpose of this paper as well as our work with Chaim Bentorah Ministries is to give the Christian a tool which will not only help in their study of the Word of God but encourage them to examine the Word of God word by word, letter by letter.

Examples of Gematria Use

The most obvious question is how do you compare the numerical value of various Hebrew words? Is there a catalogue or a book that gives every word in Hebrew its numerical value. As of this time, I have not found any such book. However there was a computer expert who did develop a program that did catalogue every word in the Hebrew Bible and assign its numerical value. This listing can be found on the website, www.biblewheel.com. Our website www.chaimbentorah.com offers a link to this site. All one needs to do is go to the page hosting the Gematria and type in

[327] Ibid., pg. 29.
[328] Ibid.

the numerical value of the word you are researching. The site will instantly bring up all the Hebrew words used in the Hebrew Bible that shares the same numerical value.

Love אהבה.

The Bible teaches, "thou shalt love thy neighbor as thyself: I [am] the LORD."[329] The word for love here is *ahavah* אהבה. It would be important when studying this verse that we understand just what God means by *love* and why does he concluded by saying: "I am the Lord."

Our first most logical step would be to check the Lexicon and there we find that the Hebrew word for love אהבה *ahavah* means *love*.[330] Well, that really does not help much as love means many things in our English language. There is parental love, spousal love, friendship love and we even apply love to a sexual act which we call *making love*. So it is really important to have some idea what is meant by love here and it seems our lexicons really do not help that much.

If we look at this word esoterically we will find that it is spelled Aleph - God, Hei - God's presence and Beth - heart. So from the letters we can discern that love comes from God and is an example of God's presence and originates from the heart. That may explain why the verse concludes with "I am the Lord" as this is a love that comes from God and is meant to be shared with your neighbor.

We can go a little further by looking at the numerical value of the word love אהב. The Aleph = 1, the Hei = 5, the Beth = 2 and the Hei = 5. Thus the word *love* has a numerical value of 13. People who love each other are joined in that love. Love needs to be returned. The *ahavah* 13 of one person and the *ahavah* 13

---

[329] Leviticus 19:18, KJV.
[330] Davidson, pg. 9.

of another person would total 26. If we look for other Hebrew words that have a numerical value of 26 we find the sacred name of God YHWH יהוה (Yod = 10, Hei = 5, Vav = 6 and Hei = 5). Thus when man joins himself in love with another, it is there that God chooses to reside.

Bread לחם

Jesus said that he is the *bread* of life. Do we find something divine in the word *bread* לחם. The Lamed speaks to us of receiving something from heaven into our hearts The Cheth teaches us of a binding together with God and the Final Mem speaks of the hidden secrets or knowledge of God. Thus the letters tell us that from the bread לחם we receive a teaching or knowledge from God that will bind ourselves to Him so that we may enter into the secrets of His heart. When the Jews left Egypt God sent them a daily miracle of manna or bread from heaven. For forty years the Jews learned that their daily bread was a gift from God. This gift from heaven, Lamed, helped to bind them to God's Cheth and led them into the knowledge of God, Final Mem, that God was a God who would care for them.

We can go a little further with the Gematria. The Lamed = 30, The Cheth = 8, and the Final Mem = 40. This gives us a total of 78. The name of God YHWH has been shown to have a numerical value of 26. Say you multiple 26 by 3 and you get 78. The three could represent the Father (26) who sent His Son Jesus (26) to earth and at his Baptism He was filled with the Holy Spirit (26).

Soul נשמה

"In the beginning God created the heaven and the earth. This duality is mirrored in the creation of man. The earthly portion is the dust from the ground, formed into our material body. Corresponding to the heavens is the breathe of God, which infused us with His Spirit and allowed us to be created, "in his image."

The numerical value of the soul *neshamah* נשׁמה is 395 (Nun = 50, Shin = 300, Mem = 40, Hei = 5). The word for heavens is hashamayim השׁמים which has a numerical value of 395 (Hei = 5, Shin = 300, Mem = 40, Hei = 5). This indicates that there is a relationship between heaven and the soul. One interpretation would be that death does not mean extinction, what came from the dust will return to the dust.[331] The soul, however, is identical with heaven. It came from God and it will return to God to spend eternity.[332]

And You Shall Return תשׁבו

I have been very careful to not refer to the esoteric nature of the Hebrew Alphabet as hidden messages, secrets or codes. That is simply not the case nor the intended use of the esoteric nature of the Alphabet, however, you cannot avoid wondering if God may not have buried a secret message in His Word which can show up when you read the Word of God esoterically.

Before the twentieth century some rabbis felt that the Scripture did predict when the Jewish people would return to their homeland. They looked at the passage, *In the year of this jubilee ye shall return every man unto his possession*[333] and took the word תשׁבו *tashuvu* which means and you shall return and examined this word esoterically.

These are the words chosen to be inscribed on the Liberty Bell. In Leviticus 25:13 this word seems to be spelled incorrectly.

[331] Ecclesiastes 3:20, KJV.
[332] Blech, pg. 129.
[333] Leviticus 25:13, KJV.

Grammatically it requires another Vav ‎ו and should be spelled תשובו. The rabbis asked why the Vav was missing. They could not answer that until after World War II. Taking the word as it is presented in Leviticus 15:13 תשׁבו they determined its numerical value to be 708 (Taw = 400, Shin = 300, Beth = 2, Vav = 6). When the Jews write the year they ignore the millennia which in this case would be 5,000. On the Hebrew calendar this would present the year of 5708 as the year that the Jews would return to their land. By coincidence on the Julian calendar that would be the year 1948, the year that the Jews did indeed become a state. Yet, why did Scripture leave out the Vav? Was it so that God could provide a word of comfort to the Jewish people who were living in exile and allow this numerical value of Tashuvu to pin point the year of their return? For had the Vav been included the return would have taken place six years too early according to this prophecy. Perhaps that was the case, but the Jews feel God would not allow a word to be deliberately misspelled just to fit a time frame. They conclude that the missing Vav which equals six represent the six million Jews who did not return because they perished in the Holocaust.[334]

Is The Gematria and Letter Meanings an Acceptable Practice

Is all this just a coincidence, are we just reading into these coincidences like some conspiracy theorist? Perhaps this is so, we cannot be sure. When I visit churches or Christian organizations as a guest speaking I give everyone an envelope containing a Scripture verse with a study on the particular Hebrew words in that verse. Everyone gets a different verse. I often attend meetings of people who consider themselves to be a part of the prophetic movement. I am careful to say that I am not a prophet, just a student

---

[334] Blech, pg. 214-215.

of ancient languages, but if they happen to get a verse and a word that speaks to a specific need they have they can decide if it is a prophetic word or not, as far as I am concerned I am only sharing these little studies as a learning tool. It never fails that I have more than one person approach me after the meeting to say that the verse and word I shared with them spoke to a prayer, need or something from which they were seeking a word from the Lord. I simply remind them that I am not a prophet, if there is anything prophetic the prophetic is within them and between them and God.

As far as I am concerned these coincidences are just the nature of the Hebrew language and if it fits, and provides a deeper understanding, then I will use the Gematria and letter meanings as a tool and encourage others to try these tools in their own personal study of the Word of God. If they find it fits, great, if not, then don't try to put a square peg in a round hole, just more on.

Gematria and letter meanings are to this day an acceptable form of gaining knowledge and insight either from Biblical texts or from Hebrew names or words among many Jewish scholars. It is frequently addressed in the Talmud, and has been considered a legitimate form of interpretation among Jews who study the Scriptures and, more generally, as an acceptable form of learning messages from the Hebrew language.[335]

As expressed throughout this paper I am not suggesting that just because two words have the same numerical value or the suggested meanings behind the letters that this will give us an accurate understanding of an ancient word. I am only suggesting that from my experience with the *coincidences* that I have described as well as the common attitude of Jewish rabbis and scholars over many generations that the ancient Hebrew language and the structure of its Alphabet would suggest that the composition of

[335] Shore, pg. 29-30.

the root of a word is meaningful and if two words share the same root they must somehow be interrelated. In other words there is a design built into this language and it could very well be a design by God Himself.

Chapter Four
WORD PLAYS

What Is A Word Play

Word plays in the Hebrew Bible are an accepted linguistical phenomenon among Bible scholars, although many tend to overlook them as they can be very complex in nature and there is a tendency to read more into a passage than was intended by the writers. However, word plays do exist and are often referenced by many notable scholars and commentators. Yet we are dealing with the inspired word of God not just a piece of ancient literature. If there are word plays, God had intent behind the word play and it therefore becomes more than a literary exercise, but a study on the part of a Christian and a dependency upon the Holy Spirit to discern if the apparent word play does indeed exist and if it does just what is the message behind the word play.

Word plays are common in all languages, we have many such word plays in English. They are often used as literary devices to further explain a matter, make a poetic statement or more often to just add humor. Puns are the greatest example of such word plays. For instance a word may have different meanings. There is an essential oil named *Joy* because its fragrance creates a euphoric feeling. Hence one may make a play on the word *joy* by confusing the context. You could say, "Old Chinese proverb says, 'He who puts oil on top shelf, jumps for joy.'" The word *litter* has a meaning of throwing trash on the ground. The word *fine* means paying a penalty or something that is good and appropriate. Hence you can make a play on words by saying, "I saw a sign, 'Fine for Littering' so I thought it was a good place to throw my trash." *Litter* is a reference to a cat defecating so you may ask, "I f I throw a cat out the car window, is that cat *litter*?"

There are puns where words sound alike, for instance, if one asks what a Hoosier is, you could reply, "An upright vacuum cleaner." You are speaking of a product known as a Hoover which sounds similar to Hoosier.

Hebrew has a number of different types of word plays. For instance there is the alliterative type. Alliteration is the repetition of the same sounds or of the same kinds of sounds at the beginning of words or in stressed syllables of an English language phrase such as Peter Piper Picked a Peck of Pickled Peppers.[336]

For instance in Song of Solomon 4:4 we have, "Thy neck [is] like the tower of David builded for an armory, whereon there hang a thousand bucklers, all shields of mighty men."[337] You have the word talpiyyot לתלפיות which is rendered as *armory*. This produces the alliteration with the words for *thousands* אלף 'elep and *hang* תלוי taluy.[338]

There is also a type of word play in Hebrew called parallelism. This is where a single word bears two different meanings where one meaning parallels what precedes, and the other meaning what follows. For instance in Song of Solomon 2:12 you have. "The flowers appear on the earth; the time of the singing [of birds] is come, and the voice of the turtle dove is heard in our land."[339] The word *singing* is *zamar* זמר which also means *pruning*. The first meaning of *singing* refers to the turtle doves and the *pruning* goes back to the flowers.

---

[336] Dictionary.com, alliteration.
[337] Song of Solomon 4:4, KJV.
[338] Noegel, Scott B. Puns and Pundits Word Play in the Hebrew Bible and Ancient Near Eastern Literature (CDL Press), 2000, pg. 138.
[339] Song of Solomon 2:12, KJV.

Something that is not often considered is that Biblical writers often engage in bilingual word play. For instance Isaiah 10:8, "For he saith, [Are] not my princes altogether kings?" The word used for princes *sar* שַׂר is a pun on the Akkadian word *sarru* which is the word for king.[340]

For the most part these word plays are just interesting poetic devices and really add no real depth to our understanding of a passage. Then too, like with all literature, we can enter into a classroom debate over the meaning behind the word play or if there is really a word play to begin with.

Esoteric Word Play

For the sake of this paper I would like to introduce the idea of word plays using the esoteric nature of the Hebrew language and Alphabet. For instance, we see in the story of Esther that her Hebrew name was *Hadassah* הֲדַסָּה but her Persian name was *Esther* אֶסְתֵּר. Esther was a derivative of the name of the Near Eastern goddess Ishatar[341] and is a Persian word *satar* meaning star.[342] Hadassah comes from the root word *hadas* הֲדַס which means *myrtle*. My study partner pointed out that the myrtle plant is shaped like a star. So we do see a little bilingual word play on Esther's name. However, can there be an even deeper play on the name Esther and Hadassah. It is very possible that God is telling the entire story of Esther in her name. The name Esther אֶסְתֵּר is spelled Aleph – God, Samek – to be hidden, Taw – truth, and Resh – turning away. In other words *God* hid the *truth* of Esther's Jewish heritage so He could use her to *turn away* the wrath of Hamon. The Hebrew people knew their Queen was really Hadassah הֲדַסָּה which is spelled Hei – the presence of God,

Daleth – a doorway, and Samek – protection, shelter, support. Embodied in Hadassah was the *presence* of God and He would use her as a *doorway* to His *protection, shelter and support.*

Another interesting play on words used by esoteric rabbis is showing how shared letters suggest a shared meaning. For instance the word *kever* קֶבֶר means *grave.* Esoteric rabbis look at this word and see that if they rearrange the letters to form בֹּקֶר *boker* they have the word for morning. The very word for grave *kever* קֶבֶר is telling us that our final resting place is but the *morning* of our new existence with Jesus in heaven.[343]

Let's take a word from Scripture in Isaiah 61:3, "To appoint unto them that mourn in Zion, to give unto them beauty for ashes."[344] A former student of mine pointed out that God simply took the word for *ashes 'eper* אֵפֶר and rearranged the letters to *pe'er* פְּאֵר which is the word for *beauty.* Using the same letters only rearranging this God turns our beauty to ashes. You will find rabbis throughout Jewish literature doing this very same thing with Hebrew words to enhance their understanding of God's Word. But we are not finished yet, lets rearrange these letters once more to rapha' רְפָא and that gives us the Hebrew word for *healing.* God will not only rearrange the letters to give us beauty for ashes, but he will also continue to rearrange the letters to heal us of all the wounds that are associated with these ashes.

We can still go further if we look at the how all this is going to take place. We have three letters which teach us of ashes, beauty and healing. How does God heal us from the ashes and turn it into something beautiful? He does it with the Aleph א, his power; through the Pei פ our speaking words of the Resh ר which is repentance. With mouth confession is made unto salvation.[345]

---

[343] Blech, pg. xii.
[344] Isaiah 61:3, KJV.
[345] Romans 10:10, KJV.

CHAPTER Five
THE THREE NECESSARY CONTEXTS IN TRANSLATING FROM SEMITIC LANGUAGES

The Approach

At this point we face a serious question which is usually put forth by those who hold a King James Version only position. Their position is that the Word of God is precise and perfect and therefore there must be some standard by which we can say, this is really what God intended to say. We live in a very scientific and technological culture where two plus two must always equal four. Therefore in our Western thinking, there can only be one translation and rendering from Scripture if the Bible is truly the inspired Word of God.

This became a real issue when the Revised Standard Version of the Bible came out with Isaiah 7:14 reading, "Behold a young woman shall bear a son."[346] There was a tremendous outcry among conservative Christians that these revisionist were changing the Bible. Some even suggested a hidden agenda to discredit the Bible as the inspired Word of God and to declare that Jesus was not virgin born. Actually the word used in the Hebrew is *alemah* עלמה which means a young unmarried woman or a female child. Generally a young unmarried woman or female child was a virgin

---

[346] Isaiah 7:14, RSV

so you could render the word as virgin. Yet, the emphasis is on being unmarried and is not necessarily a reference to ones virginity. The word in Hebrew for virgin is *betulah* בתולה[347] which is not used in this passage. The argument is that the Septuagint uses the word *parthenos* which is a word in Greek that generally means a virgin.[348] Needless, to say this created much controversy. The argument centered on the use of the word *alemah* which some scholars insisted never means virgin and some insisting it could be used for a virgin. There is no definitive proof as to how the word *alemah* was used during the time of Isaiah. For one thing the context is clearly speaking of an event which was to occur in the lifetime of Isaiah yet, the New Testament in Matthew states that the birth of Jesus many centuries after the death of Isaiah is the fulfillment of this prophecy.

This is a problem in our Western scientific mindset but would be no problem for those of a Semitic mindset as they could easily see the use of the word *alemah* to mean a young unmarried woman having a child during the time of Isaiah and she would not have to be a virgin and then seeing a double meaning for a future event speaking of the birth of the Messiah and using the word *alemah* in that case to mean a virgin.

The point is, that in translating the Bible we have to have an Eastern mindset and not a strict Western technological mindset. There is no question that we need to address our translations in light of its proper syntax, grammatical use, cultural and historical significance as well as traditional understandings. However, in doing this we will still never be sure of an absolutely correct rendering unless we take a position like the King James only position that God gave us the King James Bible and that is the Authorized version where every rendering is correct.

---

[347] Davidson, pg. 125.
[348] Benton, Lancelot, edit. The Septuagint with Apocrypha (Hendrickson Publishing), 1986.

The only problem here is that our English language is in a constant state of change and words take on new meanings, different shades of meanings and nuances as time goes by. Thus, even the King James Version must and does go through various revisions and how can we be sure those revisions are correct. Yet we are faced with the problem of many different translations of the Bible and some which contradict each other.

Here I would like to revisit an earlier chapter in this book and refresh our thinking on an earlier thought. Let us look again at Song of Solomon 3:9 "Thou hast **ravished** my heart, my sister, *my* spouse; thou hast ravished my heart with one of thine eyes, with one chain of thy neck.[349] In its context this verse is speaking of King Solomon who is describing the effect that his beloved has upon him. With just one glance of her eyes she has ravished his heart." Now we generally make the association with God as King Solomon and us as the beloved. So it is reasonable to say that just once glance or one indication of love toward God and we *ravish* His heart. The word in Hebrew for ravished is לבבתני *libabethini*. The King James Version of the Bible renders this word as *ravished*. In our twenty first century thought the word *ravished* carries almost the idea of ransacking or rapping. Is this what we do to God's heart when we look to Him in love?

When you look at the nine different words that I listed earlier you find that they are all similar in some way, they all suggest some form of emotional response from God when we look at him with love. Yet each word expresses a different degree of response. Depending upon one's personal experience, educational background and level of maturity, each one of the nine different renderings could be interpreted differently by different people. A romantic minded person may view the expression, *charmed me* to represent a sense of pleasure and delight on God's part.

---

[349] Song of Solomon 4:9, KJV.

To someone who has a more mystical outlook on life they may view the expression *charmed me* as exerting some sort of mystical or spiritual influence over God. So it would be virtually impossible to express *libabethini* in an English word where everyone in the English speaking world would walk away with the exact same idea of what happens we express our love to God.

Actually when you consider this word in its Semitic root it you will find that it comes from the idea of tearing bark from a tree.[350] This is why the one version has a seemingly unrelated rendering of *wounding* the heart of God. For when you tear the bark off a tree you are exposing its phloem layer which is like the circulatory system of our body. The tree is now open to diseases and pestilences. You are not only wounding the tree you may be killing it by tearing the bark from the tree. So what this version is suggesting is that when we express our love to God He is opening up His heart to us and making Himself vulnerable to us, giving us the ability to wound His heart or break His heart. That is a far cry from capturing God's heart or charming His heart. Yet, they all carry the basic same idea only expressing different levels of emotions.

Bible translators for organizations like Wycliffe Bible Translators or United Bible Society, know and understand this problem when trying to translate the Bible into languages of cultures that are not as sophisticated as our culture. As one translator indicated, words are not limited to one single meaning, but their range of meanings extends over to other fields, thus allowing for what is known as *linguistic creativity* and yet this basic truth appears to be ignored in the actual practice of communication and of translation.[351]

---

[350] Bentorah, Hebrew Word Study, A Hebrew Teacher Explores the Heart of God (Westbow Press), 2013, pg. 3

[351] Tepox, Alfred, The Bible Translator, Vol. 52, No. 2 (Reading Bridge House), April, 2001 pg. 217.

We cannot really come to a conclusion with regard to the word *libabethini* in that we cannot know what the correct rendering really is or if any rendering that does not agree with the rendering of one accepted authorized version of the Bible, such as the King James 1611 Version, is a mistranslation for even the KJV word *ravish* carries a different meaning to different people. There is one other possibility and that is that every translation is correct. Each translation was the result of scholars who took great care in their translations and prayerfully considered every word they translated. Perhaps we should consider the fact that maybe this was part of the design of the Hebrew language to make it ambiguous so that it could reach people on every level emotionally.

This is why I propose that we not only consider the technological and scientific skills involved in translation such as the grammar, syntax, and historical background but that we also add an emotional context to our renderings. We need to use our scholarship and linguistical knowledge in our translations. But for the translators, that is usually where it will end. When it comes to putting a rendering into an emotional context that is left up to the individual Christian. One cannot readily depend upon some scholar having a theology and relationship with God that is unknown to the reader, dictate to the individual reader just what he does to God's heart when he says that he loves God. That is really a matter between the individual Christian and God.

Hence, we can go only so far with the scholarship, but we must move on to the second approach to translation and that would be to put it into an emotional context. However, when an individual does this on his own, he must apply a third approach and that is the revelatory work of the Holy Spirit.

Thus, when we study the Word of God our first approach is to see what the scholars have to say about certain words in the Hebrew. From there one must apply his own emotional context and in doing so he must seek the revelatory work of the Holy Spirit in his own life. Thus, I propose three approaches to the study of the Word of God:

1. Technical input
2. Emotional input
3. Holy Spirit input

Implementation

The Torah was originally written without any indication of the beginning and the end of each verse, or with the proper vocalization of the words as there was no punctuation or vowels. Hence Genesis 1:1 would be written as follows:

בראשיתבראאלהימאתהשמימואתהארץ

In the beginning God created the heavens and the earth. There are no vowels or punctuation. If we were to write this in English it would it would appear as: **nthbgnnnggdcrtdthhvnsndhrth.** Even knowing what it says without the vowels and punctuations it would still be very difficult to read in English, yet that is what a translator would face with the original Hebrew. The question is asked, why was the Torah written this way? Rabbi Bachyei gives us what I believe is the best answer. He says that this is in order to enable us to discover numerous and varied new meanings by punctuating and vocalizing the Torah in ways other than the standard ones, and by grouping the letters into new words, different from those which appear in the Torah scrolls. In this way, hidden worlds are opened and revealed to us. For instance the first words of Genesis 1:1 are בראשית ברא – *In the beginning God created.* However, there letters could be divided in a different way to read: ברא שׁ יתברא which would mean, *It was created with (or* *for) the head.*[352] The sages would argue that this is not creating a new meaning but only giving deeper understanding, opening hidden worlds to us in the study of the Word of God. In other words it was created by God and for God.

Our society is very dependent upon scholarship and experts. We will rarely venture forth without some scholarly or expert advice. Our form of leaning in the West is to sit before an expert and let them lecture us while we take notes and any discussion is usually for clarification of what the expert is teaching us. I have found that many classes in a Bible college are nothing more than a discussion of what other people who have certain acceptable credentials have said. Yet, these people that are discussed have the same amount of the Holy Spirit as everyone else.

The teaching method of the Near East and Semitic cultures, particularly among the Hebrews was to ask a teacher a question and the teacher often responded with a question of his own guiding the student to discover the answer for himself. It is this mindset that one must have to utilize the three approaches to translation of the Word of God. Christians are very good at talking about the revelation of the Holy Spirit and allowing the Holy Spirit to guide us into all truth, but if our conclusions do not match that of the experts, then we question or we are fearful of our own conclusions. We need a balance of expert input in our studies but also the right to question the experts conclusion in light of one's personal revelation of the Spirit of God inside of them. As Rabbi Bachyei presented, sometimes there is hidden knowledge outside the standard explanations. As Shakespeare said: "There are more things in Heaven and Earth, Horatio, than are dreamt of in your philosophy"[353]

The word of God is a well that will never run dry. If we approach the Word of God with the confidence of the Holy Spirit

[352] Glazerson, pg. 12.
[353] Shakespeare, Hamlet, Act I, Scene 5.

within us to reveal His truth to us, then we can move beyond the insights of the scholars and begin to apply our own emotional context and the revelation of the Holy Spirit. When this happens a whole new world of Bible Study opens up to us, the Word of God then becomes relevant and personal and we begin to really hear the voice of God.

Before we begin to implement these three approaches to personal Bible study we must first remove ourselves from our Western thinking that we are personally inadequate to study the Word of God without expert input. If we can truly believe that God can speak to us personally through His Spirit we are then ready to implement the three approaches to Bible study.

Preparation for Study

We find that the ancients Hebrews as with many in the Near East lived a very holistic life. By holistic. I mean this in the philosophical sense. Holism is the theory that whole entities, as fundamental components of reality, have an existence other than the mere sum of their parts. In other words our study of the word of God must encompass mind, body, soul and spirit. The Bible commands us to love the Lord God with all our hearts, soul and might.[354] That is to say we need to love the Lord holistically, with our mind, body and soul. We do this without even realizing it. We go to a church which often has a beautiful sanctuary, that appeals our sense of sight, we listen to beautiful worshipful music that appeals to our sense of hearing, we are sometimes asked to hold hands with other believers or lay hands on others appealing to our sense of touch, sometimes fragrances are diffused appealing to our sense of smell and we share communion appealing to our sense of taste. Worship is meant to be holistic, using all our senses.

---

[354] Deuteronomy 6:5, KJV.

We speak of a *quiet time* with the Lord. As Christians when we hear this we think of a special time, perhaps in the morning when it is quiet, before the rush of the day, and we are alone and we spend that time in prayer, meditation and study of God's Word. What we are doing is putting ourselves in a position to give our entire being to God. We shut out the noise of the world that would distract our hearing, we go off to a garden, maybe, where the fragrances of the flowers create a restful sensation in us. We look around at the beauty of God's creation, appealing to our sense of sight. In other words a quiet time is a time when God can have control of all our senses. Our quiet time is a very holistic and holy time with our Savior.

As with any form of study, we must prepare ourselves, we must find the right environment and atmosphere to begin our study and we must allow ourselves plenty of time in our study so we can search out the truths of God in Scripture and hear His voice.

Beginning Your Word Study

Most students make the mistake of just picking out a Hebrew word and finding its various usages throughout the Old Testament and coming to a conclusion as to the meaning of the Word. There is nothing really wrong in this approach, but it must be remembered that one Hebrew word has a wide range of meaning. The Hebrew language is more contextual than most languages which are more definitive. All languages must consider the context in which a word is spoken and all words have some definition to them. However in many languages which have a few hundred thousand words, you only need to check a dictionary to know its meaning and in some cases where there are multiple meanings, you will need to consider the context in which the word is used.

However, Classical Hebrew has only about 7,500 words and one word can have a variety of meanings and hence the context that the word is used in is extremely important. It is for this reason that my Hebrew Word Study books have four volumes and each word is defined within the context of a particular verse rather than just publishing a Word Study book that just list the words with its various usages and meanings.

One must remember that there is a strong difference between the Greek of the New Testament and the Hebrew of the Old Testament. The Greek is a very precise language, it is the language of mathematicians and scientist. The Greek is so precise that I can take a phrase like *The son saw the man* and switch the words around to *The man saw the son* and the meaning will not change. The Hebrew, however, is a very ambiguous language. The syntax is not as precise, thus I can rearrange the words *The son saw the man* to *The man saw the son* but in Hebrew you cannot be sure who saw who and if anyone saw anyone in the first place. Hebrew is the language of poets, it is an emotional language, a language of the heart first and the mind second.

Also, we need to keep in mind that the Greek New Testament was written over a period of only one hundred years where the Old Testament spans a couple thousand years. A word used in the Book of Genesis may not have the same meaning as the word used in the Book of Malachi as words do change and take on new or more specific meanings over a period of time. I have an old *Life* magazine from 1950 which has an article entitled, *The Gay Secretary of State*. Obviously if an article was written in the twenty first century with that title we would fully expect a story much different than the one written in 1950. The word *gay* has undergone significant changes in just fifty years and now that word is even being abandoned in our language as we move into this twenty first century as it is taking a new and derogatory meaning for those to whom the word would apply. Thus, one must consider the evolutionary process that a word takes on and consider the fact that a word may have an entirely different meaning and emotional value when used with David as opposed to Moses.

We cannot just use the same exegetical principles with the Old Testament as we do with the New Testament as we are dealing with an entirely different language spread over a different time period.

This is another reason that my word studies are presented in a devotional format. By doing this I am presenting my word study not only from the context in which the word is used but by using a devotional format I am also addressing the emotional context as well. Thus I would encourage anyone doing a Hebrew word study to first choose a verse of Scripture rather than a word or find a Scripture verse that the word they are interested in will be found. Then they should proceed to define this word within the context of that verse.

The Technical Understanding of a Hebrew Word

This first step in doing a Hebrew Word study is the traditional approach and that is to examine the word from a technical aspect. One must determine the grammatical use of the word. Knowing if the word is a verb, participle, noun, or infinitive is very important. If it is a verb one should be able to determine with the use of a Lexicon the form of the verb, that is whether it is in a perfect or imperfect form. Also if it is a verb the Lexicon will tell you if that verb is used in a Qal form as a regular verb, or is in a causative form as a Hiphal, an intensive form as a Piel or as a reflective in a Hithpael form. These are all things one would learn in the first year of Hebrew in a Bible college or seminary. By your second year you will be learning proper rules of syntax which is extremely valuable in your study. However, all these grammatical functions have been explored and explained in many commentaries which can be found on the internet. Anyone interested enough and is willing to spend the time can find all the grammatical applications they need to know through the works of these learned and excellent scholars and commentators. It is doubtful that if you took two years of study of Hebrew in a seminary that you would be able to make any new discovery that has not been found by Hebrew scholars with more years of experience than you have. If you do I would question your understanding of Hebrew grammar. My recommendation is that unless you intend to write an academic paper on some grammatical function of a certain passage of Scripture, don't waste your trying to learn all the fine points of grammar. God on line and compare all the different studies that have already been done grammatically and chose what is makes sense to you.

If what you really want to do is discover what the Holy Spirit is trying to say to you in your own personal devotions, then a word study which you can accomplish without years of academic training may more to your desires.

The next thing one needs to do is consider the historical and cultural context in which the word is applied. As indicated earlier a word used in the historical context of the Book of Genesis could have an entirely different context in the Book of Malachi. Take for instance the passage in Exodus "And thou shalt command the children of Israel, that they bring thee *pure oil olive beaten for the light,* to cause the lamp to burn always. "[355] If we truly believe the Bible to be the inspired Word of God with every word written for a purpose, then we need to ask, "Why does God specifically say *pure oil olive beaten.*

Let us look the word *beaten.* In application of grammatical principles we learn that word *beaten* is very interesting. In Hebrew

---

[355] Exodus 27:20, KJV.

it is the word *kathith* כתית which is the noun form of *kathath* כתת. [356]
As a noun it would be *the beaten* or *the beaten oil.*

We must also ask, why is this even in the Bible, what purpose does it serve me as I do not worship in a tabernacle today and I have little use for olive oil. Jewish tradition, however, teaches that we are to look to the tabernacle for a model of our spiritual living. In the studying of its structure and its furnishings we can learn a lot about the structure and furniture of our own life.[357] Well, if that is the case we can conclude that just as the children of Israel were only to bring the *beaten or crushed oil* to the tabernacle, we are only to bring only our *beaten, crushed selves to God.*

Yet, there still must be more. To discover the spiritual significance behind this passage and how it can relate to the "structure and furniture" of our own lives, we need to examine the historical record regarding the process of purifying olive oil and why this olive oil is specifically to be beaten. Again, in our modern times we have the benefit of the internet which will open up to us a world of understanding with regard to these little details of ancient life. In this case by looking at a popular commentary on line I learned that this was not the olive oil that was your conventional oil produced from the grinding of a mill, but it had to come from the olive of the tree free of lees and dregs and had to be beaten with a pestle in a mortar and not ground in a mill so it would be the purest oil. When ground in a mill the stones were broken and ground and so the oil was not so pure. In other words the purest oil from the olive came from being beaten and it is a much more difficult process in obtaining oil than it is from grinding the olives.[358] This is the idea behind the essential oils. The essential

---

[356] Davidson, pg. 398.
[357] Holzkenner, Rochel, http.//www.chabad.org/prashah/article; The Oil of the Soul.
[358] http://www.biblehub.com/exodus27:20 Exposition of the Entire Bible by John Gill [1746-63].

oils differ from you standard run of the mill oil as the techniques to obtain 100% pure oil is a more difficult and costly process but the end results is a more natural and pure oil, hence much more powerful in scent and other usages. Thus, the use of a beaten oil teaches us that when we are crushed or beaten it is done to bring the light of God. Perhaps that is what the Apostle Paul meant in II Corinthians 4:7-12: [7] *But we have this treasure in jars of clay to show that this all-surpassing power is from God and not from us. [8]We are hard pressed on every side, but not crushed; perplexed, but not in despair; [9] persecuted, but not abandoned; struck down, but not destroyed. [10] We always carry around in our body the death of Jesus, so that the life of Jesus may also be revealed in our body. [11] For we who are alive are always being given over to death for Jesus' sake, so that his life may also be revealed in our mortal body. [12] So then, death is at work in us, but life is at work in you.*[359]

What God wants to do is to put us through that type of difficulty that has the potential of *kathath(ing) (crushing)* us so that He can strip away all that trust in ourselves so that the world can see our trust is in God alone. He wants to strip us of all those lees and dregs to make our faith *pure* in Him. Pure faith, like pure oil, is the most lasting and most powerful. This information about the oils is easily found on the internet today. Don't be afraid to use our modern technology.

The Esoteric Approach

Up to now we have taken the traditional approach to a word study and found some depth and personal application through our use of the technical understandings of the word *beaten* כָּתִית. Yet, this book is not your traditional presentation on Bible study, I am seeking to present a new dimension to our personal study

---

[359] II Corinthians 4:7-1, NIV

by introducing the esoteric application to our study of Hebrew words. Taking the word kathith כתית (beaten, crushed) we find that it is spelled Kap which represents an empty heart that needs to be filled with the Taw – truth coming from the Yod, messenger from heaven so that we may be able to truly Taw – praise God. That pure oil, oil that has had all its impurities beaten and crushed (kathith כתית) out of it gives off a pure light in the tabernacle to God, just as God will allow all our difficulties in this life to beat and crush all the impurities out of us so that our hearts (Kap כ) may be filled with the truth of God (Taw ת) that comes from heaven (Yod י) to open us up to true praise to Him from our hearts (Taw ת).

The Emotional and Revelatory Context

We have two possible meanings of the word kathith כתית, it could be a *beaten one* or a *crushed one*. Both tend to have a slightly different meaning in English. The question is which one would you apply in your own private translation. When you check other translations you find even more options, you could be the *pressed one, one extracted by hand,* or *a virgin oil.* How do you decided which is the correct rendering? You must decide which is the correct rendering for you and your personal situation. Sometimes after a difficult day I come to God feeling like I am the *beaten one.* At that time that is the correct rendering for me. Every so often I receive bad news that *crushes* me so I come to God as the *crushed one.* Depending on my emotional state at the time, that will guide me to the rendering that I will use in my personal translation. A week or month later, I may be facing a difficult decision and I feel *pressed* on all sides, at that time I would use the words *pressed one.* All are correct translations, all have a personal application.

However, there is one other element to be applied, that is the revelatory function of the Holy Spirit. Choosing the various meanings behind the letters and choosing the appropriate English word is like our old high school locker combination lock. A lock will have just thirty five different numbers. Yet you must choose a combination of three numbers from the thirty five in proper sequence to open the lock. There are literally thousands upon thousands of possible combinations. So it is when you use the esoteric Hebrew, there are multiple meanings behind each letter and multiple possible English words. One must apply the right combination to open the lock of your heart. How do you know which combination is the proper combination? I explained earlier, "And let the peace of God rule in your hearts, to the which also ye are called in one body; and be ye thankful."[360] The word *rule* in the Greek is *brabueto* which means to umpire or arbitrate. You do not need an umpire to call "out" when everyone knows the player is out, you need to umpire to call the close ones. You keep applying the different combinations of meanings to each letter until that little witness in your spirit, that little sense of peace comes over you and then you know the Holy Spirit umpire has given you a personal message from God.

---

[360] Colossians 3:15, KJV.

CONCLUSION

I have often said that American Christians are Biblical illiterates. We have more Bibles than any nation in the world, one of the highest degrees of literacy in the world and yet Christians spend very little time studying the Word of God. Every year pastors pass out little pamphlet called *Read Through the Bible in One Year* and challenge the congregation to read through their Bibles in one year following a certain format. Few can actually follow through with the program and those that do consider it a great accomplishment to actually be able to read through the whole Bible in a year's time. Yet, these same people will take a popular novel that is longer than the entire Bible and read through that in one week, sometimes losing sleep as they stay up at night to finish another chapter. These are the same Christians who will announce every Sunday their great passionate love for God.

I recall hearing the story of a woman who met a man a party. She was attracted to him but when he said he was a science fiction writer, she lost interest. She not only hated science fiction, she did not feel a writer was a very good prospect for a future relationship. However, this writer was persistent and before long they were dating and then engaged to get married. The night this woman was engaged she sat up in bed pondering this man that she had fallen in love with and wondered just how much she knew of this man. She wished there was some way she could just get to know his inner thoughts and his heart. Suddenly she realized she had a copy of his book that she never read. She went to her bookcase, dusted off the cover and began to read his science fiction book. She not only read through the entire book that night, she read through the book every night for the next few days. Now, did I not say that this woman hated science fiction? Just what would prompt her to lose a night of sleep reading through a science fiction book and not only that but to re-read the book every night for the following days? The answer is simple, she fell in love with its author.

The reason so many Christians do not read their Bibles is because they have not really fallen in love with its author, but how can you fall in love with someone that you do not know? The only way to know and understand Him is though His Book that He has written for us.

Another excuse I hear from people as to why they do not study the Bible is that it is too difficult to read. They tell me that I am a Bible teacher who has taught Hebrew, Aramaic and Greek. That I have advanced degrees in Biblical languages so naturally I will understand what I read, but they are just uneducated and nothing in the Bible makes sense. My response to that is that I have studied the Bible for thirty five years in the Biblical languages and there is much that does not make sense to me either, however, that does not keep me from studying the Bible.

There is another story of a salesman who paid a visit to a client who was a florist. As the salesman sat in the florist office waiting for his client to gather some papers together he examined his bookshelf. One the shelf was one very thick book, the size of a dictionary and it had one name for the title, *Roses*. The salesman said out loud, "How could anyone write so much about one flower?" Without missing a beat, the florist instructed the salesman to read the first line in the first chapter. He did and in that one sentence we find the secret to understanding and studying the Word of God. It said; "If you love it enough, it will reveal its secrets."

Again, I am brought back to the key to studying the Word of God, if you love Him enough, you will have no problem spending four, five hours or more a day studying His Word and if you do love Him enough, He will reveal His secrets to you in his Word.

What I am offering in this paper is meant for those who love God enough but cannot seem to go any further in the depth of their study than referencing a commentary or Lexicon. For those who love the Lord God with all their heart, soul and might, I am only offer a tool that will allow them to go deeper into the word of God. A tool which will take them just a little bit further after having read all they could find in commentaries and on line and have completed their technical study of a verse or Hebrew word. It is a tool which will challenge them to take the next step and put that verse or word into an emotional context and then to meditate on it and allow the Holy Spirit to do His revelatory work to give them a personal message from God.

Is there a Divine design within the Hebrew language? Did God really put a built in commentary in each Hebrew word which can be decoded by using the meanings behind the Hebrew letters? Did God design the Hebrew language to bear all these associations and relationships to similar words and structures? Did God build into each word a numerical value that would correspond to other words with the same numerical value to give a person a deeper understanding of His Word? Maybe so, may not. Maybe these are all just coincidences as many liberal scholars would like us to believe. I personally find that when I pray and place my faith in God, coincidences happen, when I stop praying and stop believing, coincidences stop happening. Just given the benefit of the doubt that this book is only presenting something that can be answered by coincidences, then the discoveries of these coincidences have helped me find a deeper, more satisfying relationship with God and a hunger to study and read His word.

During the middle ages, Jewish families would actually sit around as a family and use these esoteric tools to study the Word of God. It was sort of like a family bonding time, similar to what families do when they play board games together. Even the input of children would be taken seriously as they believe God could speak through children just as well as an adult and you do not need years of education or training to do this.

Christian families struggle with having a family devotional time which rarely amounts to nothing more than one parent doing all the talking or teaching. If families could take just one passage of Scripture and examine each word esoterically, it could be like a game as it was in the middle ages with each family member trying to unlock the right combination of meanings and numerical associations.

As to the question of whether the esoteric structure of the Hebrew Alphabet is of Divine design or the creation of man, that is a question of which we will never find a conclusive answer. However, one thing is certain, these coincidences do turn one's attention to the Word of God and that cannot be such a bad thing.

Is there is a danger in taking the esoteric structure of the Hebrew Alphabet too seriously? There is indeed, just as there is a danger in taking any study tool used in the Word of God too seriously. There is an old story in the Talmud of a rabbi who took three students into Sod (the deep mysteries of God). In the end, one student died, one lost his faith and the other went insane. Only the rabbi who had the purest heart returned from the journey unharmed.

As a Bible College teacher I have had students seek the deep mysteries of God without a pure heart. One was convinced that to get answer to prayer all he had to do was follow a certain formula he felt he discovered in the Bible. When his prayers went unanswered he lost his faith, left the ministry and to date has not returned to his former faith. I had another student who sought the mysteries of God. He studied day and night and became convinced that there was some inherent power in invoking the Hebrew name of God, YHWH. He soon reached the point believing that anyone who did not use the Hebrew name of God YHWH or the Jewish name of Jesus Yeshuah were not true believers and indeed would go to hell. Before long he became convinced that he and only the small group of followers who thought like he had the real truth and all of Christendom were deceived by Satan and doomed to hell. Many consider this former student of mine to be insane and considering his delusions of grandeur even I questioned his sanity. Then I had another student who through his study of the Word of God became convinced God called him to enter a very dangerous situation, totally ill-equipped, and untrained. He went only believing that the angels would protect him. Against all advice he took what he felt was a step of faith and ended up losing his life. Just as the rabbi lost his three students to a loss of faith, insanity, and death, the same can easily happen if we enter into any form of Biblical study without a pure heart and motives.

What I have presented is called by some as mysticism because they claim its origins are with Jewish mystics. However, if they study Jewish mystics they would discover that in the true sense a Jewish mystic is only a person seeking a relationship with an unseen God. If that makes me a mystic, so I am. However, I do not believe there is any inherent power in the Hebrew letters, but I do believe there is a power in the Word of God, the Bible and I offer nothing more than the *Old Time Religion* which was good enough for my fathers and it is good enough for me, I just simply want to find ways to swim in some deeper waters and discover the treasures that my fathers who did not have the internet, modern archaeology, modern linguistical science and other tools available to us today at their disposal.

BIBLIOGRAPHY

Alter, Michael J. *Why The Torah Begins With The Letter Beith.* Jason Aronson, Inc. 1998.

_____. *Babylonian Talmud, Seder Kodashim.* Soncino Press. 1938.

Ben Nachman, Moshe Rabbi. *Bamben Commentary on the Torah, Exodus.* Shilo Publishing House. 1971.

Ben Jacob, Ha-Kohen Rabbi. *Explanation of the Letters.* Paulist Press. 1986.

Benner, Jeff A. *Ancient Hebrew Lexicon, Ancient Hebrew Alphabet Chart.* Virtual Bookworm Publishing. 2005.

Benton, Lancelot (ed.) *The Septuagint and the Apocrypha.* Hendericks Press. 1988.

Bentorah, Chaim. *Hebrew Word Study, A Hebrew Teacher's Call to Silence.* Westbow Press. 2012.

Bentorah, Chaim. *Hebrew Word Study, A Hebrew Teacher Explores the Heart of God.* Westbow Press. 2012.

Bilton, Nick. *Disruptions: Brain Computer Interfaces Inches Closer to Mainstream.* New York Times. April 29. 2013.

Blech, Benjamin Rabbi. *The Secrets of Hebrew Words.* Jason Aronson. 1991.

_____. www.dictionary.com

Davidson, Benjamin. *The Analytical Hebrew and Chaldee Lexicon.* Hendrickson Publishing. 2007.

Donne, John. *Meditations XVII Devotions Upon the Emergent Occasions and Several Steps in My Sickness.* 1624.

Elliger R. and Rudolph W. *Biblica Hebraica Stuttgartensia, Exodus 4:10.* Deutsche Bieggesellschaft. 1975.

_____. *Electronencephalogram – EEG.* www.webmed.com.

Finkel, Avraham Yarkov. *The Great Chasidic Masters.* Jason Aronson. 1992.

Fish, Solomon. *Midrash Hagadol on the Pentateuch.* Manchester University Press. 1940.

Fitzpatric, Sonja. *The Pet Psychic.* Berkley Publishing. 2003.

Gill, John. *Exposition of the Entire Bible._www.biblehub.com/exodus.*

Ginsburgh, Yitzchak R. *The Alep Beith Jewish Thought Revealed Through the Hebrew Letters.* Jason Aronson. 1991.

Ginsburgh, Yitzchak R. *The Hebrew Letters.* Gal Einai Publications. 1992.

Glazerson, Matityahu Rabbi. *From Hinduism to Judaism* Himselsein Publishers. 1984.

Glazerson, Matityahu Rabbi. Trans. S. Fuch. *Letters of Fire.* Kest-Lebovits, Jewish Heritage and Roots Library. 1984.

Glazerson, Matityahu Rabbi. *Hebrew the Source Language.* Yerio Hasafarim. 1987. Glinert, Lewis. *The Joys of Hebrew* Oxford University Press. 1972. Grimby, Shona (ed.) *Encyclopedia of the Ancient World.* Taylor and Francis. 2006. Haralick, Robert. *The Inner Meaning of the Hebrew Letters.* Jason Aronson. 1995.

_____. *Helps Word Studies* Helps Ministries, Inc. 1987.

_____. *History of Writing.* www.historian.net./HXwrite.htm.

Hoffman, Edward. *The Hebrew Alphabet.* Chronicle Books, Inc. 1998.

Hoffman, Joel. *In the Beginning A Short History of the Hebrew Language.* New York University Press. 2004.

Holzkenner, Rochel. *The Oil of the Soul.* www.chabad.org.

_____. *Holy Bible King James Version* Thomas Nelson, Inc. 1976.

Hooker, Richard. *The Hebrews A Learning Module.* Washington State University Press, 2005.

_____. *Jewish Encyclopedia* Vol. 1 Funk and Wagnalls. 1906.

Kaplan, Aryer. *Gems of Rabbi Nachman.* Yeshivat Chasiden Breslov. 1980. Kaplan, Aryer. *The Bahir.* Jason Aronson. 1995.

Kemp, Martin. *The Heart in Christ to Coke How Image Became Icons.* Oxford University Press. 2011.

Lainier, Elias. *The Metaphysics of the Hebrew Alphabet.* Jason Aronson. 2003.

Leverhoff, Paul. (Trans). *The Zohar.* Soncino Press. 1978.

Lehrman, S. (Trans). Midrash Rabbah. Soncino Press. 1983.

Lewis, C.S. *Mere Christianity,* Chapter 8 The Great Sin. Harper and Row. 2009.

Louw, Johannes and Eugene Nida (ed). *The Greek-English Lexicon of the New Testament Based on Domains. Vol. 1.* United Bible Societies. 1989.

Magiera, Janet. *Aramaic Peshitta New Testament Vol. II.* Light of the Word Ministries. 2009.

Maimonides, Moses. *The Guide of the Perplexed. Vol. I* Trans. Shlomo Pines. University of Chicago Press. 1963.

_____. *Metsudah Midrash* Metsdah Publications. 2008.

Monk, Michael Rabbi. *The Wisdom of the Hebrew Alphabet.* Mesorah Publications. 1988.

Mozeson, Isaac E. *The Origin of Speeches.* Lightcatcher Books. 2006.

Mykoff, Moshe (Trans). *Rabbi Likutey Nachman Vol. 10.* Breslov Research Institute. 1992.

Nestcott, Wynn (Trans). Sepher Yetzirah or the Book of Creation. 3rd. ed. Wescott Publishing. 2006.

Noegel, Scott B. *Puns and Pundits Word Plays in the Hebrew Bible and Ancient Near Eastern Literature.* CDL Press. 2000.

_____. *Rashi Pentateuch and Commentary.* S.S. and R. Publishing. 1976.

Ross, Allen P. *Introducing Biblical Hebrew.* Baker Academic Publishing. 2001.

Scherman, Nosson and Zlotonitz. *The Wisdom of the Hebrew Alphabet.* Mesorah Publications LTD. 1988.

Schneerson, Menachem Rabbi. *In the Garden of Torah.* Soncino Press. 1994. Seidman, Richard. *The Oracle of Kabbalah.* St. Martin's Press. 2001 Shakespeare, William. *Hamlet* Simon and Schuster. 2007.

Shore, Haim. *Coincidences in the Bible and Biblical Hebrew.* I Universe, Inc. 2005.

Skobac, Michael Rabbi. *Daniel 9 The Truth of Daniels 70 Weeks.* *www.jewsforjudah.ca.*

Steward, David. *Healing Oils of the Bible.* Care Publications. 2012.

Tate, Karen. *Sacred Places of Goddess.* CCC Publishing. 2008.

Tepox, Alfred. *The Bible Translator* Vol. 52. No. 2 Reading Bridge House. April 2001.

Vogel, Yong (Trans.) *Mishnah Sofrim* The Jewish Learning Exchange. 1983.

_____. Weekly Torah Portion. www.aish.com May 21, 2009.

_____. What is Edenics._www.edenics.org.

Wilkerson, David. *The Cross and the Switchblade* Pyramid Publications. 1977.

Wyatt, Nicholas. *Religious Text from the Ugarit* Centinuum International Publishing Group. 2006.

Young, Gary. *Essential Oil Desk Reference.* Life Source Publishing. 2011.

Zalman, Sheur Rabbi. (Trans.) *Tanya* Kehot Publications Society. 1993

FOR MORE INFORMATION PLEASE VISIT OUR
WEBSITE AT:

www.chaimbentorah.com

or write us at

chaimbentorah@gmail.com

or call us at 708-289-3691

Chaim Bentorah has a BA in Jewish Studies from Moody Bible Institute, an MA in Old Testament and Hebrew from Denver Seminary and a PhD in Biblical Archaeology. He taught Hebrew and Old Testament at World Harvest Bible College for thirteen years as well as a Hebrew language course for the Christian Center High School.

Chaim Bentorah is a resident of Cicero, Illinois where he presently teaches Biblical Hebrew, Greek and Aramaic to pastors and lay leaders in the Metro Chicago area.

OTHER BOOKS BY CHAIM BENTORAH

Biblical Truths from Uncle Otto's Farm
A Hebrew Teacher's Journey into Silence
Hebrew Word Study A Journey to the Heart of God
(to be released August 2015)

32335989R10109